Telgi

Celebrating
30 Years of Publishing
in India

Telgi

A REPORTER'S
Diary

SANJAY SINGH

TRANSLATED FROM THE HINDI BY
GAYATRI MANCHANDA

HarperCollins *Publishers* India

First published in India by HarperCollins *Publishers* 2023
4th Floor, Tower A, Building No. 10, DLF Cyber City,
DLF Phase II, Gurugram, Haryana – 122002
www.harpercollins.co.in

2 4 6 8 10 9 7 5 3 1

Copyright © Sanjay Singh 2023

P-ISBN: 978-93-5629-426-4
E-ISBN: 978-93-5629-427-1

The views and opinions expressed in this book are the author's own.
The facts are as reported by him and the publishers
are not in any way liable for the same.

Sanjay Singh asserts the moral right
to be identified as the author of this work.

All rights reserved. No part of this publication may be reproduced,
stored in a retrieval system, or transmitted, in any form or by any
means, electronic, mechanical, photocopying, recording or otherwise,
without the prior permission of the publishers.

Typeset in 11.5/15.2 Minion Pro at
Manipal Technologies Limited, Manipal

Printed and bound at
Thomson Press (India) Ltd.

This book is produced from independently certified FSC® paper
to ensure responsible forest management.

To Mandar Parab and all those friends who were my pillars of strength during my fight for the truth

Contents

Introduction by Rajdeep Sardesai — xi
Author's Note — xv
Prologue — xxi

1. The Beginning of the End — 1
2. The Investigation Report — 7
3. The Importance of the Report — 10
4. Who Is Telgi? — 17
5. Telgi Investigation Report Decoded — 45
6. My Predicament — 55
7. India Security Press, Nashik — 61
8. Mushrif and Mandar, Pune — 65
9. Waiting for the Day to End — 72

Contents

10.	The Bullet Has Left the Barrel	77
11.	Debauchery in Custody	85
12.	An Encounter with Pradeep Sawant	92
13.	Damage Control and More Damage	97
14.	Heat Rising	104
15.	Clean Chit to Commissioner Sharma	112
16.	Shoot the Messenger: Pasricha Inquiry	115
17.	Bali Report Unveiled	120
18.	Public Interest Litigation	127
19.	A Meeting with DIG Jaiswal	138
20.	And the Arrests Begin	143
21.	Remorse of the Encounter Specialist	157
22.	IB to SIT	162
23.	Arrest of Sridhar Wagal	166
24.	The Threat of November	170
25.	Commissioner Sharma's Exit and Arrest	176
26.	The Arrest of the King of Encounters	182
27.	Fall of Bhujbal	186
28.	The Nephew in a Corner	193
29.	Bhujbal's Slipper	199

Contents

30.	Satyapal's and Parambir's 'Inquiries'	212
31.	Movie on Telgi	216
32.	CBI Inquiry	220
33.	The Unresolved Questions	223
34.	Telgi Gets Me a Promotion	228
35.	Telgi Unplugged	233
36.	The Storm That Followed the Narco CD	240
37.	I Did Not See Telgi Alive after This	249
38.	Who Was He?	258
39.	Downfall of Journalism	267
40.	Order, Order …	272
41.	What Is Yours, to You …	277
	Epilogue	285

Introduction

An Example of Courageous Journalism

In the past several years, many scams have raised their heads and been quietly buried. People's names appearing on chargesheets make no difference to their social standing or political acceptance, and this is why public perception remains that the 'big ones' never get caught.

The common man's disillusionment with the system is not limited to corruption. The media has also discarded the cloak of investigative journalism and made friends with lightweight reporting, which includes hasty interviews and nothing but a few glorious photographs. In the fast-paced world of media, a small announcement becomes 'breaking news'. A news or interview being broadcast on all channels is forcefully endorsed as 'exclusive', page 3 has been turned into page 1 (with a beautiful model's comment on the annual budget splashed across the cover page), and paying reporters to cover private parties in the media are common occurrences nowadays. No wonder then that there is very limited shelf space left for investigative journalism, which is based on valid documents, good research and much running around. This is the reason why the value of the book written by Sanjay Singh on the thousands of crores of rupees' scam, the Telgi scam, is substantially high. This scam-busting book is firmly rooted in the values of traditional journalism, extracting news straight from the 'sources', fact-finding and validating those facts from all angles, observing news from different perspectives and the most crucial of all—having the courage to clash with the Titans sitting in the corridors of power. This is not hidden-camera or versified reportage, but it gives a glimpse into journalism based on information, research and soul-searching, which fearlessly asks important questions.

When Sanjay had apprised me of the report that contained the names of the senior police officials and politicians allegedly involved in the Telgi scam, I questioned him with much disbelief. 'Can a man like Telgi alone have influence on and access to so many state governments?' Sanjay's strong determination and his impressive track record as a journalist convinced me to let him work on this case. As the news kept filtering in, my belief went from strength to strength that Sanjay was about to deliver a 'maha news' that would send shockwaves through the entire police force and political system of Maharashtra.

A few days after the telecast of Sanjay Singh's report that sensationally exposed the senior police officials who had sheltered Telgi, I received a call from a 'big' minister from Maharashtra. He said, 'You will have to put a leash on Sanjay Singh's reporting. He has been asking too many questions.' The call from the minister convinced me of the stature of the report that Sanjay was working on.

The irony remains that we are still not able to ascertain the actual value of money involved in the thousands of crores of rupees' worth scam. But it isn't an easy task for those involved to escape the keen eye of the media, and the credit for this goes to Sanjay Singh for his courageous attempt. In the present realm of TV journalism, this wasn't an 'easy' news to cover. TV needed visuals. The more sensational and flavourful, the better. Blood, gore and destruction is basic fodder for TV journalism. Visuals from terrorist attacks or images of destruction wreaked by hurricanes are like a field day for TV news. From that perspective, the Telgi scam wasn't a 'sexy' story as it was not easily translated into visuals, but rather, was a fact-based piece of news. Sanjay could successfully expose the facts (on the basis of his years of experience and with the support of reliable sources) while also fulfilling his social and professional responsibilities as a journalist. I congratulate him for that.

Rajdeep Sardesai
2004

Author's Note

A Diary of My Experiences

This book is important because in it, I, the commentator, am not giving insights based on TV highlights post a match but, rather, imagine that the match is still on and I am there on the grounds; earlier, I was on the pitch where it was being played. Since this was my first-hand experience, it has been documented in the form of a diary.

In a career span of twenty-five long years as a journalist, many news reports came and went away, exposing many truths, though none quite like the Telgi scam. I went through new, exciting and terrifying experiences while covering this news. I faced the critical challenges of saam (request), daam (bribe or reward for getting work done), dand (punishment for not acceding to a request) and bhed (to create differences between people), and clashed with frightful policemen and mighty politicians who were in power. But I did not let any of it dampen my spirit and continued to chase the news like a ghost. And at the same time, strived to stay true to the ethos of journalism. This book, too, falls within the realm of that continuous effort.

It was actually written in two different eras. The first edition was penned in the year 2004 and the current, updated second edition, in the year 2021. The reason behind this was that a web series has been made based on my book. After the stupendous success of *Scam 1992: The Harshad Mehta Story*, Swapnil Ughade, a representative of Sony Liv, met me to explore the possibility of making a web series. Coincidentally, an official announcement was also made on my birthday, 4 March, that Applause Entertainment was going to produce a web series based on my book for Sony Liv with Hansal Mehta as the showrunner.

It was a matter of pride and satisfaction, as if you were to compare the percentage of books translated from the Hindi into English is much lower than the books translated from the English into Hindi. I was a novice in the world of publishing and Ram Kumar of Paridrishya Prakashan and my writer friend, Vrushali Telang, guided me through this process. Sachin Sharma of HarperCollins encouraged me to bring out an updated version of the book. I thought that was a reasonable suggestion as the first edition had come out in the year 2004 and many things continued to happen after that, until 2017. I was continuously following this case and it was important to document it, or else the book would have felt incomplete. But it wasn't an easy task as much time had elapsed.

Anyhow, documents were overhauled, I met many people related to the case, weaved the incidents chronologically into one thread. Many of the cases have reached their logical conclusions, some are still in progress, some people have since been convicted, some acquitted, some discharged, some reinstated and some are still waiting for a verdict on their fates.

One important thing here is that my intention behind writing this book was never to point a finger at a specific person or slander their character or declare them guilty. During the course of events through which the scam was unravelled layer by layer, the police personnel and political leaders who fell within the ambit of this investigation and the mention of their names in this book is based solely on police chargesheets, the investigators' statements and relevant content from media, and also the witnesses' statements. It happens many times that the allegations made in the chargesheets are not proven true and many of the accused are in the clear and eventually acquitted by the court. The same happened here as well. In this case, too, the judiciary did their work, continued to do so and the final verdict remains theirs, as always.

Anyhow, this was a challenging task. I am not hesitant to admit that the amount of effort this took was much more than it took to complete my Ph.D. When the final book took shape, I felt that my anxiety at having left the story incomplete was put to rest with this version. From exposing the Telgi scam to following up on the case and beyond, I changed many news channels but did the same work. I started with NDTV, then moved to Times Now, IBN, News X and in the end, Zee News—a long and eventful journey. During this time, TV journalism changed its character too, both technically and content-wise. The technical upgrade was a welcome change, of course, but the quality of content majorly deteriorated and continues to break records of falling deeper and deeper into the pit (without any gains in wit).

From 2004, TV journalism has embraced indecency, debauchery and cheap thrills, and has submitted to favouritism just to gain eyeballs and increased TRPs, selling its soul to the devil. Looking at the present state of widespread apathy, if a scam like Telgi or a bigger scam is exposed, three groups of journalists will arise. One that will defend it to appease their political saviours or the mandates of their management, the other will politically oppose them and a small group (which no one will care about) will remain neutral. The audience has lost faith in the neutrality of the media today, unlike in earlier times. Probably this is the reason why no one has heard of a big scam being exposed in years now.

It was serendipity that brought me to the Telgi case. It continued to expand and assumed a colossal form much later. As it was discovered eventually, the case had its tentacles spread across all states and after my news report spilled the beans about the Telgi scam, the countrywide

Author's Note

printing and selling of fake stamps was exposed in its entirety. My investigative report revealed how Telgi was eating away into the country's economy like a termite and brought the truth behind the scam before the public. In the life of any journalist, monumental, mysterious and sensational news like that of the Telgi or Harshad Mehta or Bofors scam comes only once in a lifetime.

The scam was intricately woven and had a nationwide network. It lasted for a long time and many incidents and cases overlapped, which I have attempted to put forth here in a linear narrative form as simply as possible.

This story details the journey of Telgi, a stamp scam and the journalist who endured it. Whatever bittersweet moments came to pass—incidents from both behind and in front of the camera, the emotional and mental angst, the falling from grace and the changing face of journalism, all aspects related to the news that found or did not find space in the media—I have attempted to bring them all into the limelight for the readers of this book. How successful I have been in my endeavour is best left to the wisdom of my readers.

In the end, I would like to express my heartfelt gratitude to all the friends who helped me tremendously whenever the need arose, in collating reports about the Telgi scam and shaping up this book. Thank you.

Prologue

2004

The Qualis picked up Mandar from the Jogeshwari-Vikhroli Link Road. As soon as he got into the car, he noticed an AK-56 lying next to the gear shaft.

'Is it loaded?' Mandar asked.

'Need to keep it handy,' the man behind the wheel said.

'Maharaj ... all alone ... bodyguard—' (Salaskar was known as 'Maharaj' within the Mumbai Police circles).

'There was no need.' Salaskar cut Mandar short before he could finish his question.

Salaskar put the car in gear and it slowly started gliding on the deserted road.

The encounter list of Vijay Salaskar, Mumbai's encounter specialist, was half the size of his competitors' within the Mumbai Police department but he was still held in high esteem by his peers. Unlike others, his cases included the big 'wanted' criminals, such as gang leader Amar Naik, Sada Pavle, Vijay Tandel and Bandya Adivadekar.

His competitor, the Pradeep Sharma–Daya Nayak duo, was close to completing a century. But Salaskar was an outlier, with a penchant for working fearlessly and alone on his cases, and for this, he was looked up to by his colleagues with awe and respect.

Turning the steering wheel to take a U-turn, Salaskar asked in Marathi, 'Got the book?'

'Yes!' Mandar slid his hand into his shirt and fished a book out.

Salaskar side-glanced at the book while keeping his eyes on the road. Telgi's photo was on the cover and an NDTV mic was prominently visible in front of him.

'Please don't take it along. Read it now and return it,' Mandar requested.

'Arre, how can I read it all now?' Salaskar promptly shot back.

'This book's first edition will be released at 4 p.m. tomorrow and no one can have a copy before that. I got the book on this promise only,' Mandar pleaded.

Vijay Salaskar parked his car in the parking zone at Matoshri Club. He switched on the car's dome lights and saw his mobile show the time as quarter to midnight. For the next two hours, Salaskar continued to read the book stationed in the driver's seat as Mandar snoozed next to him in the passenger seat.

The roaring sound of the car's engine coming to life disrupted Mandar's sleep. He sat up straight and asked, 'Why are you getting into this? You have no stake in this matter, everything is related to the opposing parties,' alluding to Salaskar's rivals within the police forces.

Salaskar slid the book into Mandar's lap and responded, 'That is why my seniors asked me to check what could be so damaging in this book. They feel I share a good rapport with you all.'

'What are you saying?' Mandar asked, opening his shirt buttons to hide the book underneath.

'Bhaiya wrote everything directly,' Salaskar retorted.

Mandar laughed. 'Come to the function tomorrow, I will get you a signed copy from the author.'

'Mad or what?' Saying this, Salaskar halted the car in front of the RNA Heights building.

Mandar got out of the car, opened the entrance gate and entered the building while the Qualis moved on.

Entering his apartment, Mandar took the book out of his shirt and threw it next to the TV, thinking how if his luck had favoured him, this book would have had his name on it instead of the current author's. The book that had kept the entire police department on tenterhooks, eager to learn its contents before its release.

He switched on the TV at two-thirty in the morning to watch something and the TV screen came alive, flashing the title of the book *Telgi: A Reporter's Diary*.

Around four and a half years after this incident, Vijay Salaskar was martyred while protecting the nation and fighting courageously against Ajmal Kasab and his associates during the 26/11 Mumbai terrorist attack. He was posthumously awarded the Ashoka Chakra, the nation's highest peacetime gallantry award.

1
The Beginning of the End

29 March 2003

Saturday

The day started like any other ordinary day. In my life, for sure. I was working with NDTV, which was limited to a software production house at this point and mainly worked for the 24×7 Star News channel. I had been here for the past two and a half years and exactly after one day, that is, on 30 March, NDTV's contract with Star TV was coming to an end.

Sunday was my day off, which meant Saturday was my last working day at Star News. I craved to deliver an explosive news item on my last day at work, and leave the network in style with a big bang. But there was only one story up my sleeve today.

The Swiss couple case.

It was a case of an aged Swiss couple, who were allegedly involved in the sexual molestation and abuse of young children. The court verdict on this case was expected today. There were too many TV journalists present in the sessions court besides me, and I was feeling low and unmotivated. At about 10 a.m., I got a call on my mobile from a friend in the police department, Patil. He urged me to go to the Andheri suburbs as soon as possible, and wait for the rest of the news there.

I ditched my camera unit and without letting fellow journalists catch so much as a whiff of my sudden departure, I left the court premises. In Mumbaiya slang, sneaking out like this is called kalti maarna. I called the office and asked them to send another camera unit to Andheri to accompany me. Boarding the local train at Churchgate, I covered a distance of twenty kilometres over the next thirty minutes.

In those thirty minutes, all that I could think about was what the news might be. Was I chasing a mirage? I was afraid I might miss out on both—the news that wasn't and the news that I had left behind.

Many times in my life, I had tried to sail in two boats simultaneously, and ended up drowning in the process. Worried that history might repeat itself, I was desperate to stay afloat this time. I had decided to take a chance. Committing to the ambiguous tip, I resolved not to let its intimidating consequences deter me from my decision.

Somehow, with all the distinct possibilities and uncertainties clouding my mind, I finally reached Andheri station and found my cameraman, Baba Joshi, waiting outside. I told him that we might get some breaking news today. As always, the area around Andheri station was packed with people, so we decided to hang around the highway and wait for Patil to turn up. Our car navigated through the large crowd to reach the Western Express Highway.

Baba Joshi always addressed me as Sanjay bhai. He suggested, 'Sanjay bhai, let's make head towards Jogeshwari, park our car under the flyover and rest until Patil turns up.'

I had no qualms following his lead. We turned towards the north from the highway. It was already noon by then. We were resting when we heard a loud noise like that of a cracker bursting. An afterthought followed: what if it was the sound of a gun being fired? Just then, Baba pointed towards a moving vehicle. 'See, Sanjay bhai, the Crime Branch officer's car!'

It was Bhatt saheb's car. Without further ado, we started moving towards the other side of the flyover. The exploding sound continued to rise and then, all of a sudden, there was pin-drop silence. We had crossed the bridge within two minutes and could see familiar faces around us. After covering another twenty metres, we spotted Pradeep Sharma's* unit.

---

* After registering a century in encounter cases, Pradeep Sharma was finally arrested in the Lakhan Bhaiya fake encounter case in the year 2008. He returned to police service after a prolonged absence and subsequently arrested Dawood Ibrahim's brother, Iqbal Kasker. Later, he fought the assembly elections on a Shiv Sena ticket and lost. In 2021, he was

Wearing a bulletproof jacket, Sharma was swinging an AK-47 in his hand. In a few minutes, his counterpart Daya Nayak was spotted mirroring the guru Sharma's actions. Between them, they had had encounters with more than eighty hooligans.

Meanwhile, Daya Nayak called me. 'We confronted and killed Lashkar's Western Commander Abu Sultan and two of his associates. Two of them were Pakistanis and one was a Kashmiri,' he said.

'What news flash should I run?' I asked Daya.

'You were the first one we informed,' Daya stated unequivocally.

I knew Daya would say the same thing to a few more journalists. I told him that I had been watching him from a distance, so he began sharing details. I signalled cameraman Baba to start taking the shots. While I was still approaching Daya, I spotted three corpses lying on the ground. I called our Delhi office and their instruction was to take in the breaking news.

We broadcast the news first on Phono (news on the phone). At this juncture, I spotted Sahara News Bureau Chief Mandar Parab and Zee News reporter Calvin Joshua in the vicinity. I sent the initial photographs and taped interviews with Pradeep Sharma and Daya Nayak to the office via our driver to Uplink—the method we used to send news images to our head office in Delhi via satellite.

---

arrested for planting explosives outside Mukesh Ambani's house and killing a witness.

Mandar, Calvin and I were parallelly staking our individual claims to being the first ones to break this explosive news.

In the world of electronic news, breaking news is a concept which is akin to a high dose of dopamine to keep TV reporters happy. There are mere minutes between the news releases by all channels, yet everyone claims to be the fastest horse in the race. It is another matter that the audience views the news on any random news channel playing on TV in their living rooms.

However, if we talk about encounters, this was the biggest Mumbai Police had been in, in the past year. Pradeep Sharma and his men were seen gallantly boasting about their conquest.

I was surprised to see that Sub Inspector Sachin Vaze was also present there.

Sachin had been suspended due to an allegation that he had been involved in the disappearance of an accused of the bomb blast. Parents of the suspect, Khwaja Yunus, had alleged that he had been killed in custody due to police atrocity, and later, his body had been disposed of.

Holding a revolver in one hand and a Nokia communicator in the other, he came to me and requested not to shoot his visuals. I knew that any news of his presence here despite his suspension could create trouble for him, so I instructed the cameraman not to take any visuals of Sachin Vaze. It made no difference to me, even though I was the one who had raised a big stink in the media to demand his suspension from the police force.

Sachin came to me again after some time, and asked for his visuals to be taken freely. I suspected that he had taken permission for this from Sharma, his boss. I signalled the cameraman to go ahead. Sachin hovered over the corpse of one alleged terrorist, pretending to investigate something and told me to use his visuals as I deemed fit.

It had been thirty to forty minutes since the encounter and other media crews had started reaching the site. In some time, Joint Commissioner (Crime) Satyapal Singh and Additional Commissioner Rakesh Maria made an appearance as well. Then Satyapal Singh was interviewed. The surprise was evident on Rakesh Maria's face. He was probably wondering how the entire media had reached the site so soon. I heard him asking Mandar Parab this question.

But such inane talks find no feet amidst big celebrations. I was informed that Mumbai Police Commissioner R.S. Sharma had called for a press conference at 4 p.m. to share details of today's encounter. After having been terrorized by numerous bomb blasts around the city in the last four months, this was a tremendous moment of success for Mumbai Police. There was hope of finding additional information on the encounter from the commissioner. I thought of editing the news quickly at my office and making it to the press conference just in time. The police commissioner's office was about thirty minutes away from mine. On our way back, the accolades and congratulatory messages from my bosses in Delhi were queuing up on my mobile.

2
The Investigation Report

I had almost completed the script of the news received so far and was about to begin editing, when one of my reliable sources called on the office landline. He didn't say much, but was insistent that I meet him in person immediately. He said he had big news to share. I tried to stall him, thinking what could be bigger than the news I already had in hand? I had no inkling of the news I was stalling. I had no idea that the news he wanted to convey to me would be the turning point of my career as a journalist.

My 'source' kept insisting that we meet, trying to use the emotional pull of our long-standing friendship and swearing it was supremely important for us to see each other right away. I had to give in and agree to see him. I sent the cameraman alone to the commissioner's press conference and proceeded to meet my source at the address he had given me. 'Source' is a significant word in journalism. Source means the person who shares worthy news. In common parlance, one can call them informers, too. It is pertinent for any journalist to have reliable sources, and essential for them to protect their identities while relaying responsibly the news conveyed by them. Another important aspect of the journalist–source equation is continuity, which may entail meeting the sources regularly and sometimes—if reluctantly—publishing inconsequential news just to appease them. To maintain professional decorum, I will refrain from revealing the identity of that source in this book and continue to refer to him as the source. I had no desire to see him that day, neither was I mentally prepared to hear him out.

Cursing him in my mind, I reached the designated place of meeting. He gave me a large envelope that contained a spiral-bound document—an almost 100-page long report. The top page had 'Confidential' written on it. The next page stated 'Special Investigation Team Report'. Police Deputy Inspector General [DIG] Subodh Jaiswal had been the one to prepare this report and it was related to the Telgi scam. My source knew of my distrustful nature. To win my confidence, he showed me the original version of the spiral-bound copy he had just shared with me. I placed the report inside my bag and sought permission to leave. He was surprised at my uncharacteristic lacklustre response.

He said, 'Sanjay ji, you cannot fathom the potency of this news that you just took so lightly. You are perhaps in a rush right now or so occupied with the encounter story that you cannot pay full attention to the news I shared. But I sincerely request you to read this document carefully. You will be indebted to me for life.'

I smiled at him with disdain while abusing him at the core of my heart. I thought, why offend a source? Assuring him that I would definitely give it a read, I folded my hands and politely bid him goodbye with a forced smile on my face.

To tell you the truth, many people approach me with such reports, so those papers also seemed inconsequential.

My source had probably read my mind. He threw a lopsided grin at me that translated to, 'My friend, you have no idea that you have just landed a goldmine!'

But I was so drunk on the big encounter story that anything else seemed inane and inconsequential in front of it.

I came back to the office after my meeting and edited my encounter story, which went as a bulletin on the 7 p.m. news. All of the Mumbai office was captivated by my reportage. My chest had inflated by a few inches that day (not fifty-six inches, though.)

I left the office at quarter to eight. It had indeed been a befitting grand finale—my last day of reporting at Star News. I felt immensely satisfied with the way the day had turned out. After meeting a few friends post work, I arrived home late at night. The report given by the source was still resting in my bag, untouched.

3

The Importance of the Report

30 March 2003

Sunday

It was a long morning. I slept like a log the previous night, with no tension of having to finalize a story or meet a deadline today. 'Deadline' referred to the 'time-bound reporting' we usually had to do but the break meant we were off-air for now. NDTV was starting its own news channel from 14 April. So until the launch, there was a lull. Though there was a nagging feeling, a desire within me to show some chutzpah and make the advent of NDTV in the news world memorable with some thrilling news, it would be difficult to match or exceed the impact of the huge news I had brought in on the last day at Star News.

Little did I know that Lady Luck was all set to smile upon me, once again. I chanced upon sixteen audio tapes associated with the much-publicized Bharat Shah case. The Bharat Shah case had exposed the close nexus between the underworld and Bollywood—it had unmasked the glamour in the crime world, and the crime in the world of glamour. I went on to gather enough riveting and newsworthy material and thought the tapes may unveil an abundance of sensational news, as these tapes were exclusive.

In the world of journalism, the word 'exclusive' is held in high regard and translates to adulation in the media, accolades at the office, appreciation from the bosses, etc. Exclusive also denotes that you are the sole owner of that news, which needs to be colossal and spectacular enough to attract eyeballs on TV and readers in print. It is another matter that exclusivity has changed form and shape in the last few years. The same news plays on different channels at the same time, yet some sell it with the label of 'exclusive'. A famous person is interviewed separately by different channels, and yet it is described as an 'exclusive interview' by each channel. It is tough to ascertain whether the fault for this lies with the reporter or the editor. However, the viewer can sense the deception in this whole rigamarole. I feel that the day is not far when statements made by disengaged political spokespersons and launch of some new products will also be marketed as exclusives, despite much aplomb and fanfare.

The next stage of exclusivity is 'hype'. This means overstating a simple piece of news or sometimes even blowing it out of proportion. Basically, carrying a small news story too far and magnifying it. This impairs viewers' ability to discriminate between significant and insignificant news. One can still forgive the sin of hyping a piece of news, but how does one absolve media of the sin of forcefully manufacturing news that wasn't, and turning *that* into 'big news'? If things continue to be this dismal and deceptive in the news world, then the future of TV journalism and WWF fighters will entail sharing the same audience base.

Anyway, let us come back to our original story. I had to return the Bharat Shah case's original audio tapes to my lawyer friend, who had loaned them to me, so I purchased blank audio tapes and went to another friend's home to make copies. This friend had a double tape recorder, which could record from one tape on to another. I started the recordings. Just then, a relative of my friend's arrived at his place. He was a police officer and we knew each other. I will refer to this police officer as my 'friend in uniform' henceforth, as he is still a part of Mumbai Police and so his identity must be guarded. This friend in uniform was going to play a monumental role in my media career from thereon and the whole crusade that was going to follow.

To begin with, my friend in uniform had this compulsive habit of interfering in the matters of others, and also ruffling through others' belongings—though most policemen share this despicable habit. I told him the truth when he inquired about the tapes. He didn't show any particular

The Importance of the Report

interest in them. While taking out the tapes from the bag, I had kept the Jaiswal report on a nearby table. I still had no clue about the significance of that report. By force of habit, the friend in uniform started flipping through its pages. This intrusion may have been a potential threat if it had been another journalist in question, but not him, so I paid no heed to it. I got busy recording tapes, he, reading the report, and my friend, watching TV. Three to four hours passed by without anyone realizing. No one uttered a word the whole time.

It was the friend in uniform who broke the silence. 'Bhaiyya,' he said. He always addressed me as 'Bhaiyya'. People from Uttar Pradesh and Bihar settled in Mumbai tend to get offended by this salutation, but everyone in Mumbai addresses them in this way and I had no qualms about it.

'Bhaiyya, is this report correct?' he asked as I raised my head.

'Yes', was my answer.

He asked me the same question again and I repeated the same answer. He had astonishment in his voice. 'Bhaiyya, then you have no idea how potent this report is! This is dynamite! Once detonized, it has the potential to shred the police's reputation into tatters.'

He had my attention now, and I raised my head to hear him out and the whiff of a potential story wafting from it. The friend in uniform continued to talk. 'Arre! This would not only cost Commissioner R.S. Sharma his chair, many heads will turn in the police force. You will be famous! The whole corruption nexus will be exposed! This is certainly going to be very hard-hitting.'

I was listening to him intently. He looked at my face. Being a policeman, he could see from my expression the turmoil rising within me. He stopped talking at once and asked me after a few moments, 'Have you even read this report ...?'

I shook my head.

'Don't be a fool, read it right away! You are underestimating its importance!' His voice quivered with rage.

The report had been mentioned twice in the last twenty-four hours. My source had shown the same enthusiasm yesterday. My heart was not in reading a cumbersome report. So I did what most journalists do. I read through the last four pages which gave the synopsis, citations and recommendations. That gave me a basic idea of the story. I had not anticipated it to be as sensational or important as it turned out to be.

I resolved to read the entire report. This was the investigation report of 'The Telgi Scam', written by Special Investigation Team (SIT) head, Subodh Jaiswal. By then, my tapes had also finished recording. I gathered all my things and proceeded to return the original tapes to my lawyer friend. Then I made four copies of the report and read it on the same night.

My wife and I had our usual squabble when I returned home well past midnight. Our four-month-old daughter was peacefully asleep, but my wife could not possibly get a good night's sleep without a hearty bickering. Having fulfilled her desire, I finally went to bed. We lived in a modest two hundred square feet one-room-plus-kitchen apartment. Our daughter, my wife and I slept in our living room during the day and bedroom during the night. My mother slept in the kitchen and father slept in the passage outside the apartment. Any raised voices at night filtered through the thin walls and reached everyone's ears, yet, as if bound by an unwritten treaty and universal norms of decency applicable to lower middle-class households, no one picked at the remnants of quarrels they had overheard on the previous night. Middle-class domestic lives simply carried on at a snail's pace, undeterred.

I continued to read the report well into the night. Even after reading it thrice, there were certain things I wasn't able to comprehend. But I was fully convinced by then that this was no ordinary report. By five in the morning, sleep caught up with me. I slept until late and woke up around noon, got ready and reached my office. The report had taken over all my senses. The first thing I did in the office was conduct a thorough research on every iota of information available on the internet about the Telgi scam. Nothing much came from this and the internet search felt more like one for the proverbial needle in the haystack.

I fabricated the lie that I was chasing a news story and left from office. Since I had been clueless about the Telgi scam until this point, I found myself directionless as well. It was of utmost importance for me to understand the matter first in order to decipher the finer nuances of the investigation report. I made my way to the source who had shared the said report with me. He explained the modus operandi of the scam in detail to me and I made a few notes.

Yet again, I reached home late. My wife was livid and her angry outburst led to an action replay of the scene of the previous night.

4
Who Is Telgi?

2 April 2003

Wednesday

For the next five days, I kept reading and scribbling notes about Telgi from all the resources available—newspaper cuttings, police documents, statements from police personnel, old cases, documents submitted to the courts. I even travelled to Telgi's home town Khanapur and met a few people there. There were some aspects of the story that were unravelled only later on but for the sake of narrative coherence, they need to be presented here. After a thorough investigation and stitching together all the facts, answers to some of my questions emerged, but at the same time, others came alive. This endeavour also surfaced certain probabilities that cleared the most pivotal question: who is Telgi?

Early Life

When Telgi was in the custody of Maharashtra Police, he would regale stories to the policemen watching over him. Khanapur found a prominent place in these anecdotes. Some of the tales transcended the fine line between reality and fantasy. He would narrate suspect stories about his lineage and declare that his ancestors came from an upper class, influential family, which was why his father was nicknamed 'Ladsab'. As per him, after being struck by misfortune, the family was forced to relocate to Karnataka.

Ladsab was married to Sharifa Bee as per Islamic rituals. The family lived in a village named Telgi, in district Bijapur. A son was born to them on 16 August 1959 in Miraj area of Sangli district in Maharashtra and they named him Abdul Karim. Since the family had its roots in Telgi village, the name of the village became enmeshed with his surname and identity. Later in life, he was better known as Telgi, and very few called him Abdul Karim. Abdul Karim Ladsab Telgi was indeed a mouthful. It would not be a hyperbole to state that the obscure village owes its prominence on the internet to Abdul Karim. He received his primary education at Telgi village. Abdul Karim had two brothers, named Abdul Azim (younger) and Abdul Rahim (older).

Later, the family moved to the nearby Belgaum district and started living in Khanapur village. Situated about twenty-five kilometres away from Belgaum city, Khanapur is a small town. Ladsab was a low-level railway employee at the Khanapur Railway Station. Hardly ten to twelve trains halted at this small station. Living a hand-to-mouth existence, he could barely earn enough to buy two decent meals for his family. And in the midst of all this, Ladsab contracted diabetes and a few other diseases, and suffered regular bouts of depression. A pall of gloom fell upon this already down-and-out family when he suddenly passed away one day. After his father's death, the responsibility of the upkeep and maintenance of his family fell upon the shoulders of the mother. She was barely thirty, but her grief confined her to the bed. Both his brothers became completely dependent on Abdul Karim.

Karim and his brothers studied at Sarvodaya Vidyalaya, Khanapur. The family lived miserably, struggling hard to earn enough to support the children's education and for the upkeep of the family. If you ever drive to Goa via Belgaum, you would notice that Khanapur is situated in a lush green forest. The family was occasionally able to collect seasonal fruits from this jungle, which Karim would sell either at the railway station, or to the passengers of the cars passing through the area. Despite facing all kinds of hardships and braving testing times, Karim held on to his ambition of raising his station in life and did not abandon his education. Somehow, he managed to complete school and the agenda shifted to figuring out how to do higher studies. Khanapur was a small town with no college worthy of mention. Therefore, Abdul Karim decided to pursue his higher studies at a good college in Belgaum. The commute from Khanapur to Belgaum was two hours; the diligent Karim secured admission at Gotke College, Belgaum.

Even though Belgaum was situated in Karnataka, Marathi culture and influence pervaded the campus. This helped Abdul Karim develop a multilingual persona. He would attend college during the day and sell fruits at the station at night. This wasn't sufficient to meet expenses, so he began working at the railway canteen, while continuing to sell fruits and eatables to train passengers. Despite fighting the adverse circumstances and lingering misfortune, Karim's fortitude helped him gain a bachelor's degree in commerce. This grand feat was a matter of great pride not only for Karim himself, but for the entire Muslim community of Khanapur.

Abdul Karim may have gained his graduation degree from Gotke College, but the hardship and turbulence endured by him to reach that point had earned him a postgraduate degree from the university of life. Observing the comings and goings of trains at the Khanapur railway station, Abdul Karim felt convinced that he needed a larger canvas on which to paint the grand life he had envisioned for himself. This also meant moving out of Khanapur or Belgaum to a larger city or a bigger state to test his mettle. Goa was hundred kilometres to the west, Bangalore was five hundred kilometres to the south and Mumbai was five hundred kilometres to the north of Khanapur. He had to make a choice out of these three. He ultimately chose the city of dreams that millions of ambitious people opted for. He chose the city that would refer to him as Telgi hereon.

The Blueprint behind the Bars

Entering Mumbai is easy, living here is a challenge. Mumbai grows on people over time and becomes part of their DNA, making it hard for most people to ever quit the cosmopolis. Every new person is put through a litmus test here upon arrival. Telgi, too, endured the same. Mumbai taught him how making money could compel one to run on bent knees, if they must. He barely crawled through his initial days in the city. He started working at M/s Fillix India Limited as a sales executive, but that didn't work out.

In the mid-1980s, he moved to Saudi Arabia and worked there for a few years, but his heart wasn't in it and he kept feeling like quitting, which he soon did.

Coming back to India, he resorted to odd nondescript jobs, here and there. Telgi was trying hard to get his life back on track. One thing his stint in Saudi taught him was how lucrative Middle East jobs were for Indians. He knew many agencies supplied manpower to Middle East companies and of the modus operandi of the agents involved, and also of how some people got duped in the process.

During those days, people seeking to work overseas were mandated to get an Emigration Check Required (ECR) stamp on their passport. Unskilled and uneducated people needed this stamp the most, and the ones without it were turned away at the border. Therefore, travel agents would prepare fake immigration clearance documents for labourers looking for work in the Middle East, in order to get them ECR clearance. Telgi borrowed money from somewhere and rented a shop in South Mumbai's Crawford Market to start one such travel agency under the name of 'Arabian Metro Travels'. He began offering services like sending people to the Middle East countries for work, resorting to tricks and forgery like other agencies in the trade. He learnt early on how fraudulent activities could help one earn thousands of rupees using counterfeit documents. He spared no one to make a quick buck whenever an opportunity presented itself. Soon enough, he had cemented his racket so firmly in the field that his profits grew from thousands to lakhs of rupees. But in the end, he met the same fate as any other criminal when he got caught. He was arrested multiple times on account of forgery.

Fast forwarding to the year 2017 for a moment. Police Gymkhana was located in Mumbai's famous Marine Drive area, where Dutta Padsalgikar, the police commissioner at the time, had just arrived. He preferred to maintain a low profile. One could attribute this to his two-and-a-half-decade-long stint at the intelligence bureau. He wasn't flanked by a coterie of policemen; he had come all alone. Some journalists had organized a dinner with the police commissioner for an informal conversation, and since I was a resident editor at Zee News then, my name was amongst those invited to be part of the evening. It was strange that the organizing journalists themselves were missing from the scene, delayed by the thought, perhaps, that since it was the police commissioner, he would likely arrive late as deemed suitable in his position. As a result, only two people had arrived on time, the police commissioner and I.

We began a conversation to overcome the awkwardness of the situation. I initiated it. This was our first meeting, but I used to frequently visit the intelligence bureau building at the Bandra Kurla Complex during the Telgi scam days (2003–04) to meet his predecessor, then regional head Sudhir Kumar, who Datta Padsalgikar succeeded. During the course of the conversation, he told me he had read my book (first edition, 2004) and that I had missed one vital piece of information in the book. In the '90s, when Padsalgikar was posted in Mumbai as a deputy commissioner of police (DCP), Telgi had his first brush with the law and was arrested by the officers from the MRA Marg police station, which fell under his jurisdiction at the time. We went on to discuss Telgi's predominance in those days until the organizing journalists reached the venue. Padsalgikar later rose to become Maharashtra's DGP and two years after this meeting, he was appointed the deputy national security advisor of the country.

Let us now rewind to our original story and go back to the decade of the 1990s.

In 1993, the MRA Marg police station arrested Telgi under the Indian Penal Code (IPC) sections 465, 467, 471, 420, 34 and the Immigration Act sections 3 and 24. His case file was 'Crime No. 91 of 93'. In layman's terms, this meant a culpable offence of forgery and deception by duping innocent people with false promises of sending them for overseas jobs.

Anyone landing behind bars for such a crime for the first time usually comes out with only two probabilities ahead of them. One, that they may reform completely and second, that they go on to become a bigger criminal than they were before getting caught. People like Telgi fell in the second category.

Telgi met a person named Soni in jail, who became his accomplice and crime guru. Ram Ratan Soni was a man associated with the share market and was serving a term for a case related to forgery of share certificates. Soni, a man from Kolkata, held expertise in forging documents.

According to the prosecution's case against Telgi, it was Soni who taught Telgi the finer nuances of making forged documents in jail. He encouraged Telgi to dream big and asked him to 'ditch the game of thousands and start earning crores of rupees'. Soni was the one who told him that the stamp department was the government's most negligent department and that he could begin his con there. Soni knew the tricks of the trade well and also claimed to have connections with government officials, politicians and the underworld, who could help in such work. Telgi declared Soni his guru in jail.

Soni probably didn't know back then that the inquisitive man he had taken under his tutelage would not only grow to a stature way over and above his, but also put him in his place. Little did he know that the man before him learning the tricks of the trade would go on to mastermind the biggest scams India had ever seen. The man who would not only far surpass the fraudulent work done by his guru, but who would one day be known as 'the most audacious scamster there ever was'.

While still in jail, Telgi resolved to expand his horizons. Unlike Soni, he did not want to be a frog in the well and limit his work to Mumbai. He dreamt of building a pan-India network and rule the world of document forgery. The share-related documents fraud was a lot riskier and profits were limited. For this reason, Telgi decided to forge stamp papers.

The blueprint of the largest forgery India would see was thus formed behind bars until it was ready to be implemented.

Soon enough, Telgi was out on bail.

The Arrival and Departure of the Licence

Once out of jail, Telgi began to knit the plan of establishing his pan-India crime syndicate. During this time, he took up a job as a manager of Kisan Guest House in Colaba, South Mumbai. He met the guest house owners' sister-in-law, Shahida Begum, there. The meeting transmuted into love and love into marriage. Now that Telgi had both a family and a home, he slowly proceeded to execute his scheme.

Telgi applied for a stamp vending licence at the Superintendent of Stamps office, and received it on 18 March 1994. His licence number was 12500. Telgi had sought the assistance of Samajwadi Janata Party member of the legislative assembly (MLA) Anil Gote to obtain the licence in order to reach the then state revenue minister, Vilasrao Deshmukh.[†]

When his name appeared during Telgi's narco test later, Vilasrao Deshmukh said the following to PTI: 'When Anil Gote came with Telgi's application to me, I recommended it further for licence in good faith. I just wrote "Please consider" and the Stamp Registration Office issued the licence only post due diligence as per the designated guidelines, background check and police verification.'

Once the licence was obtained, Telgi swiftly put his ponzi scheme in action. He erased the ink from used stamp papers and prepared to use them as counterfeits for resale in the open market. Then he mixed them with original stamps acquired through his genuine licence. Since these stamps were sold via an authorized licence

---

[†] Vilasrao Deshmukh later became the chief minister of Maharashtra.

holder, no one suspected any foul play. It was estimated that Telgi sold counterfeit stamps worth rupees six crore by mixing them with genuine stamp worth rupees two crore. In the first year itself. The proportion of mixed stamps was so high that complaints were filed against them at almost all the police stations of Mumbai. All investigations led to the licence held by Telgi. Around fifteen months after the licence had been obtained, on 21 June 1995, superintendent of stamps and Indian Administrative Service (IAS) officer Radheshyam Mopalwar cancelled Telgi's licence. (Later on, in his confession, Telgi stated that Mopalwar was working hand in glove with him. Subsequent to this, the Central Bureau of Investigation [CBI] made Mopalwar a co-accused in the case.)

Soni feared that this was the beginning of the end, but Telgi still had his spirits intact. His mind was prepared for such an eventuality a good deal in advance.

A Well-Oiled Machinery

Dawood Ibrahim was admired in the underworld of India for his vision and foresight. In times when Rampuri knives and musclemen ruled over gangs, he introduced the gun culture in the underworld. Instead of killing his target directly, he would outsource the job to smaller gangs or encounter specialists. Dawood knew well that he would come under the radar of the law one day and hence, had silently built an alternative empire in Dubai. In the 1980s, even before the police could take any action against him, he, along with his key gang members, escaped to Dubai and operated from there. Leaders in all fields have to be far-sighted. Telgi was the Dawood Ibrahim of forgery; he had a road map ready for the future.

He thought of printing original-like stamps to be sold by authenticated, licensed stamp vendors and thus it was imperative to acquire an authentic machine for printing. He chanced upon the India Security Press based in Nashik, Maharashtra. It printed documents like postal stamps, revenue stamps, judicial and non-judicial stamps, share transfer certificates, etc. In a nutshell, barring currency notes, all kinds of government documents were printed by the press.

First, Telgi purchased machines from the India Security Press during their junk sale. These machines were meant to be dismantled before being sold in junk, but Telgi greased the palms of some officials and procured the machines intact. He also acquired the blocks used for stamping. These blocks were mandated to be destroyed, but that did not happen. The corrupt officials of the India Security Press made the negative and positive blocks available to Telgi for money. Telgi started the operations of his parallel press, which was named Mudran Offset Printers. To ensure the smooth functioning of his scam, he created a toolkit that was named Special Points. This contained fake franking seals, embossing materials, composing letter blocks and rubber stamps. The other accessories and instruments were also arranged.

Alongside the authorized India Security Press, he started selling his counterfeit stamp papers in the market. He made slow but steady progress in the expansion of his work. Different bank accounts were opened in the names of different firms. Some of these were M/s Citizen Enterprise, M/s Prime Services, M/s Unique Services, M/s Unique Enterprises, M/s Cauvery Enterprises and M/s Sri Sai Enterprises. He hired godowns across India to safeguard his fake stamps, most of which were located in and around Mumbai.

His vendor network expanded extensively—a lucrative 20 to 30 per cent commission was offered to them by Telgi, against the standard 3 per cent commission offered by the government. The enticing margins incentivized the vendors, which augmented sales. Even the vendors weren't able to differentiate between real and fake stamps.

The top tier of Telgi's workforce comprised chartered accountants and senior marketing managers. The bottom tier included over three hundred and fifty agents, graduate sales and marketing executives, delivery teams and telemarketing teams, among others. Be it retail sale by small-time vendors or bulk supply to business houses, nationalized private banks, lawyers, real estate agents, government–private companies or financial institution contracts, Telgi's stamp sales were thriving and business was booming.

He established contact with the underworld of all areas of operation, and paid them handsomely to buy their silence. In the year 2002, Lal Krishna Advani, the minister of home affairs at the time, wrote a cautionary letter to the then chief minister of Maharashtra Vilasrao Deshmukh, about Telgi's connection with the underworld and Pakistan's intelligence agency, Inter-Services Intelligence.

Telgi managed to buy the loyalty of local police everywhere he operated, which accentuated his growth and ensured his scam could continue unobstructed. He had no dearth of money. Printing fake stamps and stamp papers was equivalent to printing counterfeit currency. He exploited all the arms of governance: politicians, bureaucrats, the stamp department and the police, treating them like his beloved mistress.

This scam created a well-oiled machinery in over a dozen states in the country, which facilitated the creation of a parallel economy which worked according to Telgi's convenience or at times in auto mode. Telgi took advantage of the autonomy of his well-established system to indulge in debauchery at dance bars.

Tables Turned—A Dance on Chance

Just as the door of Topaz Bar opened for a few seconds to let a potbellied customer in, a gust of ear-shattering music spilled out on the streets fleetingly. The music notes must have reached the ears of a police patrol vehicle passing by. But the DB Marg police personnel had thick eardrums, so the car kept moving without paying the sound any heed.

Who Is Telgi?

Mumbai's DB Marg police station holds distinction in certain matters. It is the biggest den of pirated audiotapes and CDs in India. The vast majority of fake electronics and computer parts production and sale is allegedly done here. The maximum number of cinema halls fall under this police station's jurisdiction. The country's biggest business centre of diamonds is located in this area. It is also home to the most desirable prostitutes and bar dancers of Mumbai, and there are many famous dance bars in its vicinity.

The jewel in the crown of DB Marg was Topaz Bar, the dance bar that was considered the most exclusive of all dance bars in Mumbai. Mumbai had hundreds of dance bars spread all across the city but Topaz was the most talked about and sought after, due to the top-notch dancers who performed there.

It had three dance floors for the plebeians. One could call these the open house for common people with limited money to blow on the dancers. But deep in the belly of the bar there were rooms reserved for private performances, only for discerning customers. The potbellied man from before sank deep into a sofa inside one such special room. The manager knew his taste and his deep pockets well. Topaz Bar had exclusive employment rights over the dancers, who were doppelgangers of famous Bollywood actresses, and this special customer had a penchant for these dancers. Many performed and left, but the special customer sat waiting, an ardent Madhuri Dixit fan. Then came Madhuri aka Muskaan (both fake names). Unlike other customers, the potbellied man did not blow hundreds of rupees in wads of ten-rupee notes. He blew big wads of hundred-rupee notes without any salaciousness, and with the grace of a dignified man of means.

The next day, the entire Mumbai dance bar world was abuzz with rumours and animated discussions over the hearsay: a man had blown eighty lakh rupees at Topaz Bar the previous night. He also supposedly promised the dancer a home in Rajasthan upon her retirement. Eighty lakh was a whopping amount back in the 1990s—one could easily use it to buy twenty-five kilos of gold in those days. When the hot rumour—a different amount of the money blown being quoted every time—reached Mumbai Police, their whole network became active.

Telgi had been reported to many places for forgery earlier, but he had used money to bail his way out of all such situations. The Mumbai Police had first caught a whiff of Telgi in the year 1995, when one of his rackets had been exposed.

The bar incident news spread like wildfire and Mumbai Police recognized that they may have landed a golden goose in Telgi. One by one, cases against him were registered at six different police stations in Mumbai, and then some personnel from Mumbai Police heartily milked the milch cow named Telgi.

Maharashtra's Special Investigation Team chief S.S. Puri had once shared this incident in a lighter tone. Telgi, an absconding accused in six pending cases against him, had applied for interim bail that was rejected, and yet the police had not been able to lay a finger on him. Despite the presence of investigating officers and their teams from six different police stations in the court that day, Telgi had left the courtroom unobstructed, with ease.

The police did not arrest Telgi and those investigating officers offered such unbelievably feeble excuses for his escape that one could neither trust nor wonder at, considering their flimsy origins.

One excuse was 'I had stepped out to drink water when Telgi escaped.'

The other lamented, 'I was so wrapped up in listening to the court's verdict, that I missed Telgi's escape from the courtroom.'

The third said, 'I was talking to the lawyer when Telgi went missing.' The other excuses offered were just as lousy as the ones stated above.

By this time, stamps made by Telgi were being sold like hot cakes in almost all states across India. The scam was most prevalent in Maharashtra, Karnataka, Gujarat, Andhra Pradesh, Delhi, Goa, Bihar and West Bengal. Telgi had evaded arrest so far by appearing as an inconsequential small-time scammer, just about 'managing' to make his way through. But once everyone developed a sense of his grandiosity, he became the focus of their attention. People started conniving and strategizing on how to exploit his situation in their own sweet ways.

The future outcome of this revelation was close. His mask of a small-time scammer was off. Everyone was now aware that the stories floating around for the last five years, featuring the opulence of 'Karim Lala' or 'Karim Seth' of Khanapur, were about none other than Telgi himself.

If one was to single out one act of indiscretion that caused the downfall of Telgi, it would be that one night at the dance bar.

He Scammed the World, Bollywood Scammed Him

Telgi always dreamt of owning a cinema hall, where he could watch movies of his choice at his own convenience. He was clearly a Bollywood fan. The CBI and police chargesheet records show that Telgi invested a substantial amount of money earned from the stamp scam into Bollywood. He came across Mickey Bihari one day. There are many self-proclaimed brokers like Mickey Bihari in Bollywood, who work as mediators for helping people invest black money, arrange meetings with filmmakers or make heroines available on demand. If you happen to be in or around Oshiwara in Mumbai, you will find the coffee shops swarming with groups of people passionately discussing filmmaking projects—none of these people consider their film ideas to be any less than the legendary *Sholay*. If you have money, they will leave no stone unturned to dazzle you with dreams of prosperity and how you can multiply your money in Bollywood. It was thus that Mickey Bihari convinced Telgi that he could make enormous profits by investing his money in Bollywood.

Telgi had accumulated splendid wealth by then. With great aplomb, he established a production company, Sanna Movies International, named after his daughter Sanna. He produced two movies as well. One was *Bechaini*, which was produced in the year 2000. The movie was a big disaster at the box office, resulting in a huge loss to Telgi. Next, he invested in a second movie, *Biwi Kamaal Ki, Saali Dhamaal Ki*. This film also met the same fate as the first and flopped badly. Telgi had fallen prey to Bollywood's cheating mafia and had burnt his fingers producing movies. He also realized that film production was not his cup of tea but had been duped of tens of lakhs of rupees in the process.

Telgi then decided to try his hand at another Bollywood-related business—film distribution. He acquired the distribution rights in Maharashtra and Karnataka, for the Mahesh Manjrekar-directed movie *Jis Desh Mein Ganga Rehta Hai*, which featured actors Govinda and Sonali Bendre. He again faced tremendous losses. After two years, he distributed Govinda–Raveena Tandon starrer *Ankhiyon Se Goli Maare* and yet again, faced massive losses. As per Pune Police, a floppy disk recovered from Telgi showed that he had invested approximately 11.5 crore rupees in the TV and film world in total, of which eleven crore was black money. Out of this, 5.5 crore had been invested only in one movie. There were also a few Hindi and Marathi serials in the list. The CBI also seized four bank accounts that Telgi used to conduct Bollywood-related business.

It was most intriguing how a scamster who had the entire system—politicians, the police and the underworld—under his spell could be scammed by the Bollywood mafia. Perhaps one of the reasons for this debacle was that Telgi was blinded by the glamour of the film industry and was driven by his greedy heart instead of his vicious mind while making these transactions. The result was many a failure.

Hands Smeared with Ink, Soaked in Blood

28 September 2001 was a Friday. The area surrounding Mahim Creek was busy, bustling with the typical Mumbai commotion. Suddenly, someone noticed a suspicious object floating in the water. The police and fire brigade were called, and the object turned out to be the corpse of a young man. The signs of torture were clearly evident on the corpse. There were over twenty burn marks inflicted through cigarette butts. The body bore deep lacerations caused by hard thrashing, and one haphazardly bandaged fractured foot, which had dried-up blood marks on the bandage. A case was registered at the local Shahu Nagar police station. Photos were released in the newspaper and on television, but no one came forward to claim the body and thus the police personnel performed his last rites. The corpse's clothes and photos were stored in the record room. Due to lack of evidence to successfully establish the victim's identity, the case was closed.

But the floating corpse was eventually traced to Telgi. Luck did not favour Telgi this time and he got implicated in the murder case. Nine months after the corpse was discovered, the police cracked a fake stamp racket in Pune and arrested an associate of Telgi. This associate unearthed the mystery of the Mahim Creek corpse, and the information was relayed to Mumbai Police by Pune Police. Thereafter, a police case was registered against Telgi and his associates. Until now, only cases of fake stamp papers, fraud and cheating had been registered against him—this was the first and only case of murder that ever came out in the open. A scamster known to bribe his way out of fraud cases was now suddenly an accused in a murder case. When the details of the crime were revealed in the chargesheet, it read like the script of a Bollywood movie.

The name of the deceased was Christopher Bhatti. Christopher hailed from Dandeli, a village close to Telgi's village in Karnataka. He was the sole educated and earning sibling amongst his five brothers and sisters. Christopher's relative, Arun Harly, had introduced him to his neighbour, Telgi, who offered him employment at his office in Chennai. Christopher, along with Suraj Batki, another colleague from the same office, schemed to plunder some cash from the money made through Telgi's fake stamp racket. They both drove towards Goa with the loot and cooked up a false story of having been beaten up and robbed on their way. To authenticate their story, they inflicted visible real injuries on their bodies. Then they told Telgi a sob story of how some unknown miscreants had looted one hundred eighty thousand rupees from them, but Telgi caught a whiff of their treachery. Suraj Batki was forcefully brought to Mumbai, where he confessed to the theft and also returned eighty thousand rupees. Christopher went missing. Telgi relayed a message offering truce to him through Arun Harly, and invited him to meet with him at his Cuffe Parade house in Mumbai to settle the issue. Christopher took the bait.

Telgi and his associates mercilessly tortured Christopher. He attacked Christopher with a hockey stick that fractured his leg, and his leg started bleeding. Telgi asked Arun Harly to leave and later, along with his associates, bandaged Christopher's leg, supporting it with a wooden log. Christopher died of shock from the torture. Thereafter, Telgi and his associates drove twenty-two kilometres in Telgi's car to dump the body in Mahim Creek. Next day, the high tide threw the body ashore and it was spotted by the passersby who reported it to the police. Thirteen months later, on 27 October 2002, Telgi was arrested.

However, it had still not been established that the corpse recovered from Mahim Creek had indeed been Christopher Bhatti. Experts were called from Kolkata's forensic science laboratory. Samples of bloodstains recovered from Telgi's flat, car and from the corpse were matched with Christopher's parents' DNA—his parents were called from Karnataka to identify the body in the pictures.

Finally, in November 2007, Judge U.D. Salvi declared Telgi and five of his associates guilty of culpable homicide not amounting to murder, and sentenced them to seven years' imprisonment. Christopher's parents felt Telgi's crime warranted a harsher punishment than the one he got.

This was the sole incident in Telgi's life where his fake stamp ink-stained hands got covered with human blood.

Telgi's Exit Plan

The standard modus operandi followed by all politicians is to create wealth once in power, and then channel that money into several businesses. This is the reason why many politicians from Karnataka and Maharashtra have investments in sugar mills, cooperative milk societies, educational institutions, hospitals and construction companies. They accumulate wealth to beat the clock while their time is still ripe. Politics is a game of ebbs and flows. Politicians need money to stay afloat when on the ebb and these businesses ensure regular income for them and their families.

Similarly, underworld dons divert their ill-gotten gains into the film industry, construction and politics. This is a tried-and-tested formula for seasoned crooks to safeguard their money. Telgi was a superstar in his field and had to follow the norms set by other masters. An officer associated with the investigation shared the exit plan Telgi had devised for himself when his days of forgery would be over.

Telgi was continually receiving money from the stamp scam. He didn't know how to manage that much money and where to invest it. He would spend an insignificant amount on social programmes, sporting events and the upkeep of temples, mosques and shrines in Khanapur. He would spend lavishly on his opulent lifestyle in Mumbai, at dance bars. But he felt the need for an organized outlet to invest his accumulated wealth, sooner than later. He engaged the services of two professional financial consultants to help him find the right avenues to invest his money.

Telgi went to Madhya Pradesh and became interested in the soya (soybean) business. He opened some front companies in Madhya Pradesh with Malwa International being one of them. Malwa International dealt in transporting raw soya from Indore to Bangalore for oil processing units and oil exports. The investigation revealed that Telgi had incurred a loss of 2.5 crore rupees in this exports business. He also showed interest in exporting elephant's foot or yam to Dubai, as it had a long shelf life.

In a quest to build a multipurpose empire, Telgi made a substantial investment in the petroleum product business. Under the guise of legitimate petrol production businesses, petroleum products such as naphtha, kerosene, benzene solvent were used to adulterate petrol and diesel. Telgi established front companies to do this, which were named in the CBI's FIR against him. In the petroleum product business, Telgi's name was associated with the notorious millionaire businessman Antim Totla, who was also known as Kerosene King. In the year 2003, naphtha importer Totla was questioned during the Telgi stamp scam investigations.

He was connected closely with many politicians and was arrested only later, in an adulteration case.

Telgi already had money invested in different Bollywood projects. He also aspired to buy a dance bar and construct a hospital. He purchased several benami properties in Karnataka's Belgaum, Khanapur and Bijapur, and intended to deal in commercial complexes and real estate. As per the officers associated with the investigations, Telgi had a premonition that the fake stamps scam would not last forever. He wanted to exit the scam before it backfired. Taking shelter under other white-collar businesses, Telgi wanted to spend the rest of his life as a white-collared wealthy politician and retire in the comfort of his home town, Khanapur. But his calculations went wrong and his time was sure to be up eventually. If only his plans had not gone haywire, who knows, he might even have become an MLA or MP one day.

In Jail, Forever

The year 2001, the month of October was coming to an end in a few days when the phone rang at the Bangalore police commissioner's office. The person on the line was adamant to speak only with the commissioner. The call was transferred to him. Police Commissioner Sangliana was given a crucial tip on the phone, and he immediately got into action. A police team from Bangalore was dispatched urgently to Ajmer, Rajasthan.

Jayant Tinaikar placed the phone back on its cradle and stepped out of his hotel room to breathe in some fresh air. He turned his head around to observe how Khanapur had transformed from a small suburb into a small town over the past fifteen years. He and Abdul Karim were the same age. The hotel belonged to Tinaikar's family, and he had watched Abdul Karim starve in the olden days. Then one day, Abdul Karim Ladsab Telgi had vanished from the face of Khanapur and reappeared after many, many years. Now, he was respectfully called Karim Lala or Karim Seth. Tinaikar's suspicions were aroused when he observed that not only was Telgi buying multiple properties in Khanapur, but at rates far above the market prices. Telgi's altruistic behaviour and exemplary contribution to social and religious causes were turning him into a native hero in Khanapur. Telgi's family seemed to have undergone a 360-degree turnaround, from a life of destitution to one of bathing in riches. Such abundance of wealth in such a short amount of time—Tinaikar felt there was something fishy. In the past years, he had sent written complaints about this matter to officials and politicians in Bangalore and also met them personally, but nothing had come of it.

Tinaikar read in the newspaper that Bangalore Police had arrested two people in front of Kapali Talkies in August 2001 and confiscated fake stamp papers worth fifty-three lakh rupees from them. Further investigation led the police to more stamps worth 8.5 crore. Badru and Vitthal, both the people arrested in this case, named Abdul

Karim Ladsab Telgi as the mastermind behind the stamp scam. The Bangalore Police were since on the lookout for Telgi. Since Tinaikar belonged to Khanapur, he had many informers in the town. The moment he got to know that Telgi was taking a few people to Ajmer Sharif on a pilgrimage, he called and informed the Bangalore Police commissioner immediately. He was anticipating accolades and a handsome reward in lieu of his tip.

The Bangalore Police reacted promptly and cast a net at Ajmer Railway Station to nab Telgi upon his arrival. But Telgi did not show up. Then, the police went to the famous shrine of the Sufi saint Moinuddin Chisthi Khwaja Garib Nawaz, and waited for Telgi. The team waited for him at the dargah for a week. One day, lead inspector G.A. Bawa got a tip on the phone about Telgi's impending visit to the dargah. Disguised as a Pathan businessman, Bawa reached the dargah accompanied by a local police personnel.

7 November 2001 was a Wednesday. About one hundred and fifty people were present at the dargah that day. Suddenly, Bawa spotted Telgi sitting in the middle of the crowd to camouflage his presence. Telgi was under observation for over an hour as he soaked in religious repose and looked at ease. A police operation at a religious place in the midst of a dense crowd was a delicate conundrum, but this was a now-or-never situation. Police officer Bawa knew that Telgi was also referred to as Lala. He closed upon Telgi and then addressed him as Lala. Telgi thought a known businessman had called him by his name and

drew closer to Bawa, who immediately caught hold of him then and there, and before anyone could react to what had happened in the fraction of a second, Bawa swiftly moved Telgi out of the place. Later, the police team took Telgi back to his lodge room for a thorough search. They found a suitcase filled with fake stamps. They also recovered thirty-five lakh rupees in cash, one old tape recorder and audio cassettes from Hindi movies from the room.

The police team that arrested Telgi didn't realize that they had landed a shark in their fish net. They had no clue about how widespread his network was across the country, and what the magnitude of his scam was. They realized it only on 25 January 2002, when, seventy-eight days after Telgi's arrest, the Karnataka government formed the Karnataka Special Investigation Team that came to be known as Stamp It, entrusted with the investigation of the Telgi scam in Karnataka.

This was Telgi's last and final arrest. He never saw the light of day as a free man outside jail.

5

Telgi Investigation Report Decoded

The haze began to fade after I finished reviewing the substantial research material I had collected on Telgi. The picture was becoming clearer now. I read the investigation report umpteen times and after marking the important points, moved my focus to the main scam in Pune. The Pune scam was turning out to be the 'mother and father of all scams'. At this point, it did not strike me that the process of exposing the largest financial scam the country had ever witnessed in front of people had already begun.

It is imperative to mention the significance of the Jaiswal Report here. If it wasn't for this basal report, perhaps nothing further would have happened. It became the tiny seed that grew into a mammoth tree, unearthing the biggest financial stamp scam the country had ever seen. I embarked upon decoding the Pune stamp scam and slowly, the report started opening up in front of me.

In June 2002, Pune Police uncovered Telgi's fake stamp scam of 2,300 crore, and collected accolades from the media to their heart's content. R.S. Sharma was Pune's police commissioner then. Inspector Prakash Deshmukh of Bund Garden police station was the investigative officer and S.P. Mulani was his superior, overseeing the case. Additional Commissioner S.M. Mushrif was instructed to keep a close eye on the ongoing investigation.

In October 2003, about five months after the scam was exposed, S.M. Mushrif complained of irregularities in the probe into the Telgi case. He alleged that names of five wanted accused from the initial probe had been replaced with six new people's, at the last minute, that too without any explanation whatsoever. These six names had no prior reference or records in the police case diaries.

The six new names mentioned in the chargesheet submitted on 3 September 2002 included Telgi's wife, Shahida, their daughter, Sanna and his ailing brother, Abdul Rahim. Mushrif alleged that these names had been added only to extort money from Telgi and would all have been released later due to the lack of evidence against them.

Mushrif also complained that even though he was the supervisory officer, his juniors and investigating officers were wilfully insubordinate during the probe and when he complained to the commissioner, R.S. Sharma, he refused to take any action against the corrupt juniors and advised Mushrif not to escalate the matter. He then accused Sharma of shielding the corrupt police officers.

The Pune controversy hit the roof and officers launched a mudslinging match against each other in the media. As a result, the Telgi scam case investigation was taken away from Pune Police. On 2 November 2002, an SIT was formed to carry forward the investigation, and was also instructed to examine all the allegations made by Mushrif. Subodh Jaiswal was put in charge of the SIT. Jaiswal was DIG, State Reserve Police (SRP), at the time, and the position was labelled as a punishment posting.

Besides the above allegations, questions were raised on the delay in booking Telgi under MCOCA, which stands for Maharashtra Control of Organized Crime Act (India). It is a rather prominent act formed to make special provisions and for the control of and coping with criminal activity by organized criminal syndicates or gangs, and for matters connected therewith or incidental thereto. Telgi was operating an organized crime syndicate so expeditiously that he could give big conglomerates a run for their money with his whopping profits, but due to internal mudslinging within Pune Police, booking Telgi under MCOCA was delayed.

Meanwhile, Subodh Jaiswal investigated the allegations made by Mushrif and found them to be true. The description of proceedings he recommended post the investigations are listed in the next few pages.

Inspector Prakash Deshmukh: Investigating Officer

Inspector Prakash Deshmukh of Bund Garden police station was the investigating officer till the time of filing the chargesheet. The report stated, 'Prakash Deshmukh is squarely responsible for all the acts of commission and omission in the case. Circumstantial evidence points a finger at perverse conduct, incompetence, negligence, and dishonesty beyond a reasonable doubt.'

Assistant Police Commissioner Ashok Kamble

SP Ashok Kamble of Lashkar division of Pune Police, under whose jurisdiction the Bund Garden police station came, was found to have shown signs of 'avoidance of duty, negligence and indifferent attitude towards official work.'

Assistant Police Commissioner M.C. Mulani

Grave observations were recorded against this officer. Karnataka Police had access to a recorded telephonic conversation in which Mulani had allegedly sought a bribe worth crores from Telgi. The report stated, 'The overall conduct of Mulani during the investigation was perverse, remiss, negligent and dishonest.' Commissioner R.S. Sharma also expressed doubts about the background of this officer.

Deputy Commissioner of Police Kishore Jadhav

The police station conducting all the investigations fell under the jurisdiction of Deputy Commissioner of Police (DCP) Kishore Jadhav. The report stated that DCP Kishore had a poor level of understanding of law and was not up to the task of ensuring proper supervision of the case. The acts of incompetence and mala fide were abetted by him in this case, a fact which amounted to misconduct.

Deputy Commissioner of Police Jai Jadhav

DCP Jai Jadhav had taken over the investigation from PI Prakash Deshmukh in September 2002. Jadhav did not give appropriate attention or further investigate Telgi's linkage with the India Security Press. He had taken handwriting samples of Telgi but did not send them for handwriting analysis. He did not send the stamp papers seized from Telgi's company's clients for examination.

Deputy Commissioner of Police Vasant Koregaonkar

This officer did not take adequate care in supervising the panchnama to ensure that all documentary evidence was seized properly. The unnecessary haste shown is inexplicable. He did not bother to bring on record the names of certain accused disclosed to him in case diaries.

Additional Commissioner S.M. Mushrif

Pune's additional commissioner Mushrif supervised the investigations of the case under the oral orders of Pune commissioner R.S. Sharma.

Mushrif made the following statement during the probe on the allegations made:

'Once I realized I was deliberately ignored and vital developments of the investigation were intentionally kept away from me, I distanced myself from the investigation from the second week of August 2002 ... The increased proximity between investigative officer Inspector Prakash Deshmukh and Commissioner R.S. Sharma led to insubordination from Deshmukh, and he refused to obey my orders ... I made no attempt to lodge a complaint against Deshmukh to the Commissioner as it would have been a futile exercise.'

The SIT refused to acknowledge the statement made by Mushrif. The report stated, 'Responsibility for the poor supervision has to be taken by Mushrif as he was in a position to ensure that preparation of documents, writing of the case diaries and collation of the evidence collected during the course of investigation was carried out properly.'

One positive observation recorded about Mushrif's conduct set him apart from the other police officers. Jaiswal clearly stated in his report: 'If Mushrif had not raised the issue of bungling in this case, the case would have died a quiet death at the trial stage as the investigation has not been carried out properly. The same fate as the other cases registered against Telgi in Maharashtra in which he was not arrested and allowed to abscond with connivance of police force in the respective areas.'

Joint Commissioner M.S. Mahesh Gauri

Mahesh Gauri was held responsible for the inordinate delay in invoking MCOCA in the case.

Commissioner R.S. Sharma

There were deplorable observations made about Sharma in the report. The report stated, 'Failure to insist upon timely application of MCOCA provision to the case by Pune Commissioner was a strategic error which was further compounded by issue of an inadequate order confining its application against only two persons by the Jt. CP. The additional availability of time would have been beneficial for the investigation. There is no logical reason on record to explain this act of error/omission.'

Regarding application of MCOCA, the report stated, 'The fact that this situation was allowed to arise can only lead one to conclude that Pune commissioner R.S. Sharma let the situation drift to the detriment of the case.'

R.S. Sharma had stated orally before the SIT about the dubious credentials of assistant commissioner of police (ACP) Mulani. Despite knowing about the credentials of ACP Mulani, however, he allowed him to accompany him to Bangalore for the investigation, which is inexplicable. Further, nominating Mulani to the new investigating team is also inexplicable as Mulani had already been transferred out of Pune for allegedly playing a dubious role in the case investigation.

When Additional Commissioner Mushrif made allegations, they would definitely have had some basis. The least that could have been done by Sharma was to immediately find the truth in the allegations. Failure to do so was also termed as inexcusable in the report.

Similarly, clarification was also orally sought from the commissioner on his alleged statement before Mushrif, while giving instructions to carry out the probe: *'Ek karodpati ki aurat ko aaropi nahi banaane ki kimat bahut jyaada ho sakti hai'*. Which means the price of not listing a millionaire's wife as an accused can be substantially high.

Recommendations of the Jaiswal Report

Jaiswal made the following recommendations in his report, out of which five were regarding actions against R.S. Sharma.

1. Inspector Prakash Deshmukh and ACP Mulani should be suspended and departmental action should be started against them on charges of misconduct and criminal negligence.
2. Minor penalty punishment and non-executive posting for ACP Ashok Kamble.

3. DCP Kishore Jadhav who was found guilty for criminal negligence and misconduct should be dealt with major penalty proceedings and should be transferred to non-executive post. He should also be sent to the Police Training Institute for training in investigation.

4. Minor penalty punishment for DCP Jadhav and DCP Vasant Koregaonkar.

5. This investigation was extremely crucial as the case has national ramifications and financial structure of Maharashtra and India was being underlined systematically. Hence it is for the government to consider appropriate action against Add. CP Mushrif, Jt. CP Mahesh Gauri and Commissioner R.S. Sharma for their several acts of omission and commission.

6. The specific economic offence in cases like these needs to be referred to specialized agencies like the local Crime Branch, CID or CBI for organized police investigation.

7. Telgi was the main accused in all cases registered at Mumbai, Nashik, Thane, Kolhapur and Pune but the stamp scam continued to flourish due to lack of action against him. Another reason was Telgi's nexus within the stamp department, Mumbai Police and local police departments.

8. Unfortunately, the government is yet to ascertain how this scam affected the nation's economy. The

option of the franking machine proved reductant too. Cases of fake stamps surfaced in Karnataka despite having franking machines in place. The investigation revealed that Telgi and his associates had done preparations to commence counterfeit franking operations.

9. The security at Nashik-based India Security Press is highly erroneous. Strict corrective measures and actions recommended that it was the centre and Maharashtra government do not face further revenue loss from here in the future.

Author's Conclusion

Jaiswal recommended direct action against the accused juniors and also suggested the line of action, complete with the punishment. While he recommended action against three senior officers (including R.S. Sharma), he remained silent about the line of action, as all of them were Jaiswal's seniors in rank.

6

My Predicament

7 April 2003

Monday

Contrary to my nature, I started turning up late to work. Since the new channel was starting on 14 April, some new reporters had also been hired. There were still a few days left for the channel operations to begin. Two new bosses had been sent from Delhi, Srinivasan Jain for English and Abhigyan Prakash for Hindi. Both got all reporters busy in creating a pool of news reports that would come handy upon the launch of the channel. In journalism jargon, this is called creating a 'story bank'. I was asked to create my own stock but I had no desire to do the work. Since the centre of power was the head office in

Delhi, which had dispatched two fine commanders to rule the roost, I had no option but to bow to their orders.

I tried all the tricks of the trade to put together the next two stories and since I was a senior reporter, the expectations from me were higher. I had to prove my compatibility with the team in order for the entrusted to successfully establish their kingdom. Have you heard the famous Hindi saying that loosely translates to 'darkness befalls the city where the king is incompetent and vegetables cost the same as precious cashews …'?

But all this while, I continued to collect information on my main case.

My predicament was complicated and a big turmoil was brewing within me. The 'atom bomb news' had fallen into my hands when there was no channel to air it on. I often had visions of the ripples this sensational news could have caused had our channel been operational then. But there were still a few days to go until the channel started. I was constantly getting agitated over the probability of other news channels getting their hands on the report before I could break the story. Would I miss getting credit for breaking the historic news based on this report, despite being the first journalist to have got his hands on it?

Was this boat destined to drown so close to the shore?

I was certain this piece of news was set to be a defining milestone of my career as a journalist. If the news broke under my name, every time it would be referred to in the future, so would my name.

A premonition about my report being on an equal footing with news like that of the Bofors scam, share market scam, Jain hawala case and the latest Tehelka tape case, in the high corridors of journalism, kept my spirits soaring.

Prone to daydreaming, I turned into the quintessential Don Quixote, thinking day and night of my success. But the inane fear of the Telgi report reaching someone else before my story broke continued to claw at my heart. Trouble often accompanies happiness like a bride's dowry at her wedding.

The next two days passed wrestling with this conundrum. I mulled over the report multiple times and started collecting vital information from senior police officers. One salient feature of TV news is its representation through visuals supporting the news item. This is an art that involves technical expertise. To cross this hurdle, I resolved to visit the India Security Press in Nashik to collect the visuals for my news story.

For some reason, I was convinced this would be a good start. But securing consent from the office for this trip became an issue. TV journalism is like cooking two-minute instant noodles. If a journalist requests time to research for a story, the editor considers it to be a lame excuse for enjoying paid leave. Now, this mindset is detrimental to the ethos of journalism, but who really cares about that. Quantity is given precedence over quality of the news in this fast-paced world. Every reporter is only as good as his last news telecast. He may break his back over a story for a week, put his blood, sweat and soul into bringing a story together, but in case the news is not delivered by the eighth day, he is declared a nobody by the resident editor. This is ominous for the future of journalism. In the eyes of a reporter, the resident editor is like an overseer keeping a hawk eye on the daily wagers—the reporters—who must toil to earn their daily bread and butter.

The reporter feels neither respect nor deference towards his senior. In an ideal world, the reporter–editor relationship is akin to a student–teacher bond. However, in reality, the chasm only widens between them. The reporter feels the editor applies the 'condom theory' of use and throw to them as their juniors, and dispirited, inevitably starts hunting for a new job. The editor is ultimately responsible for the reporter's bleak outlook towards his workplace, as he holds higher accountability owing to his age, experience and seniority. If the editor is so inclined, he can mentor and guide the journalist in the right direction. Unfortunately, very few editors share that mindset in the news industry. Everyone, including reporters, editors, news channels and newspapers, eventually suffer at the hands of this collective mayhem, but the biggest casualty of the whole chaos is the spirit of journalism. The anger and resentment flows through organizational veins like a slow poison and inadvertently turns into professional animosity.

I have always felt that in the last eight to ten years, newcomers have been embracing the world of news as a viable career option, as opposed to being driven by a commitment to journalism. I was constantly in conflict with my idealism and feared that I might lose the battle.

I needed to get approval from my bosses to go to Nashik, for which I'd have to share with them the nature of the news story I was chasing, and that seemed very challenging. It was then that I thought of Rajdeep. Rajdeep Sardesai was NDTV's editor-in-chief. It was a big risk. In case Rajdeep refused my travel sanction, no one in NDTV would grant me permission. But somehow I felt Rajdeep would understand my predicament.

I called Rajdeep on 7 April and sought his permission to travel to Nashik to cover an eve story. Rajdeep responded in a perturbed voice, 'Listen, Sanjay, do go if it is an exclusive story. We are quite stressed here as the launch is approaching. We need a big story. A story to launch the channel, with NDTV's name associated with it.'

'I have just the right story for that', was my response.

Rajdeep asked in a hopeful tone, 'Is it that big a story?'

'I can't share details, but it is a *huge* story. I just need your permission to travel to Nashik for now. The storyline is clear in my head but I will share it only at the final stage.'

There is an old saying, 'If you want to keep a secret, do not tell your boss about it.'

'All right!' Rajdeep took a deep breath. 'Go ahead, but get something solid.'

'I don't want to tell anyone about it right now. Please keep this to yourself. No one in the Mumbai office can know anything either,' I pleaded with him.

'Looks like you have hit a jackpot.' There was thrill in Rajdeep's voice this time.

'Yes!' I responded.

I made an excuse at the Mumbai office, and skillfully roped in my favourite cameraman Sanjay Rokde to accompany me. Rokde and I have worked together for years. He was like an elder brother and mentor to me. I learned a lot from him during my entire journalism career, and always addressed him as Dada Rokde.[‡]

[‡] In Maharashtra, the elder brother is addressed as 'dada'.

7

India Security Press, Nashik

8 April 2003

Tuesday

Early morning, we started our journey from Mumbai to Nashik in our official car. Nashik, an old city, is located about 180 kilometres from Mumbai. We reached there by afternoon and headed straight towards the press road. Nashik has two old government presses. One where currency is printed and the other, the India Security Press, where all kinds of stamp papers, share certificates, etc., were printed. The latter was our destination.

We reached the India Security Press, located two kilometres further in from the main road—the entire stretch was the property of the press. Any kind of photography was prohibited there and if caught, one could find themselves behind bars. We surveyed the situation and returned to the building after half an hour. Rokde started taking visuals of the press building from the car itself. We were mentally prepared to escape if anyone approached us and became suspicious. The driver kept the car engine running, anticipating the same outcome. We stepped out and then returned to the same spot after clicking a few more visuals.

Then I approached the gate of the India Security Press. I asked the security guard to connect me to the general manager. Someone allowed me to speak to the general manager's office at the security post by the gate.

'This is Sanjay Singh … a journalist with NDTV,' I introduced myself. 'I want to speak to the general manager'.

'What do you want?' the voice on the other side demanded.

I responded, 'I am doing a story on stamp scams and I want to speak to your manager in that reference.'

'Sir is busy,' the voice gave a terse response.

I was adamant. 'I will wait. Let me know when he is expected.'

'Sir won't be able to meet you', came the empty answer.

'Okay,' I said, disheartened. 'Give me his phone number. I will call him from Mumbai.'

'There is no phone here.' At this, I realized something was amiss.

I said, 'Okay, I will find the number from the directory. You tell me your boss's name.'

'I cannot tell you his name', said the voice on the other side.

I was getting frustrated. 'Why! Are you his legally wedded wife that you cannot take his name?' Whoever was on the other side of the phone said nothing, so I asked him again, 'Okay, tell me your name, at least.'

'I cannot tell you,' he said.

'Why? Your parents forgot to name you when you were born?' I was certain that something was fishy.

When no response came from the other side, I threatened him. 'Your days are up, you rascal! You have pandered to Telgi and swindled public funds. That's why you are scared to share names.' I was deliberately trying to rouse his anger, and even cursed him with the choicest Hindi slurs so that he would step out in rage to confront us. 'Whatever your boss has done, it is going to cost him dearly. He will lose his job and also land behind bars. I will come back and deal with you then. Tell your boss it is just a matter of days. He will be arrested within a month.' I was shooting arrows in the dark.

'Sir, we are mere servants,' he whispered in a muted voice and the phone was disconnected.

I kept the receiver back on the cradle. The security guards looked at me with amazement. 'Scoundrels. All of them. They will be caught one day.' I threw a glance at the guards and highbrowed my way out of the situation. I was well aware of how miserably I had failed at my attempt, but this much was certain that high-level secrecy was being maintained at the India Security Press, possibly to cover up some high-level mess. There was something critical that was forcing them to create such interference even for routine matters.

I was having tea at a stall outside the press when a man approached me. I had noticed him near the press entrance during the altercation with the press official on the phone. He said he wanted to have a word with me. He had my ear, but then he preferred to carry out the conversation at a different location and asked me to meet him at Sayba Hotel on Bombay Naka Road in an hour. The man was there at the designated location at the time he had committed to. Disclosing his identity might prove detrimental for his career as he may still be employed there, so I will guard the secret. He shared many insights about the environment at the press and the people there, especially the general manager, Ganga Prakash. The information shared by him could not be verified, but going forward, it was to turn out to be vital for my work.

Leaving Nashik late in the night, I headed straight for Pune. The city of Pune is located about 250 kilometres from Nashik. I reached there at about four in the morning, rented a room at a hotel and was soon fast asleep.

8

Mushrif and Mandar, Pune

9 April 2003

Wednesday

We woke up at 9 a.m. and headed straight to the residence of SRP DIG S.M. Mushrif. When the news of the Telgi case first broke out, he was Pune's additional police commissioner (crime), and the suspicious involvement of corrupt policemen in the cover-up of the Telgi scam was exposed due to his efforts. It was as if the skies fell on my head when I entered his residence. I cursed my ill fate as I stepped into his living room to find Mandar Parab already sitting there. He was a journalist like me. He was also the bureau chief of Sahara News in Mumbai.

Mandar's presence threw me into a dilemma, and I found myself fighting against my wavering mind. Mandar wouldn't have come to Pune after a 180 kilometre drive just to say hello to Mushrif. My denial mindset took over. I started thinking that Mandar may have been an old acquaintance of Mushrif's and may have come to pay obeisance. But I knew Mandar well—he was Mr Lazybones and wouldn't even lift a finger without reason. He and I had known each other before we became journalists.

Mandar was two years my senior in journalism. Whereas I started straightaway with TV journalism, Mandar began his career with newspapers like *Bombay Eye* and the *Free Press Journal*. He entered the world of TV journalism with DSG TV.

His career took a leap when he joined the In Mumbai TV channel in the year 1997. This channel gained great popularity amongst the people. Mandar used to cover crime beat then, and his work made a substantial contribution to the popularity of the channel. His crime sources were better than mine. This was the reason why he was always a few steps ahead of me in his reporting. I was often envious of his achievements.

But this turn of fate had presented us two archrivals with an opportunity to work under the same roof. Mandar had joined Zee News after quitting In News. The external competition had now moved closer to home.

We worked together on many big news stories at Zee News. Later, I joined NDTV and he moved to Sahara News. We were back in the boxing ring of news. But there was no animosity between us any more. We were often spotted together and people assumed there was a deep bond of friendship between us. But the reality was something else. Inwardly, we were afraid of each other. In the cutthroat world of TV journalism, neither of us wanted to put his neck on the line.

There were gross dissimilarities between us. Mandar was highly meticulous in his life and I was disorganized. I lived a vagabond-like existence in terms of my appearance and dressing sense. Mandar, on the other hand, enjoyed the materialistic pleasures of life. I was sloppy and he was a connoisseur of the good things. We maintained a cordial relationship and neither ever interfered in the other's personal life. We maintained secrecy between us. We both had common friends, but abstained from tattling.

We both were peace-loving, good-natured and anti-establishment. Both derived great pleasure from reporting news against people in the high corridors of power or in influential positions.

Whereas I was a daydreamer, working on far-fetched news prospects based on my intuition and often failing miserably, Mandar only pursued sure-shot news, where success was guaranteed. Mandar never worked on any subject where the probability of success was less. This was the reason why Mandar was a more successful journalist than me, and this quality of his started nagging me the moment I spotted him inside Mushrif's home. Mandar was probably going through the same turmoil as me.

I rewound the past mentally within a fraction of a second. After the initial pleasantries were exchanged, we sat down. Mushrif asked if we were acquainted. I nodded my head but in response to Mushrif's next question, we explained that our concurrent visit was a mere coincidence and that we hadn't planned to come together. But Mushrif looked askance. Police personnel are, anyway, suspicious by nature. However straightforward any issue may be, they habitually visualize a twisted angle.

Our initial conversation established the similarity in the motive of our visits—we both had similar goals and were working along the lines of the same investigative report. Our eyes met during the conversation and we could gaze at each other's inner turmoil. Both were doubtful of each other. The conversation was happening with Mushrif but in hindsight, we were both busy measuring the level of work the other had put into the report.

My heart was sinking. Mandar's channel was on air, that is, it was broadcasting news already, whereas our channel's launch was still five days away. It was evident that Mandar would break the story on his channel. He would be the first to telecast all related news. He would expose the role of all the guilty policemen involved in the scam. His name would be associated with the revelation of the most explosive scam in the history of the country and here I was, so close yet so far from the finish line.

Mushrif gave us all the details related to the matter. How he was subjected to injustice, how he was made to go through abjection and humiliation. This was probably my first time witnessing a police officer feeling incapacitated in that manner. But he did not give up. Mushrif was certain that if criminal complaints were registered, misdeeds of senior police officers could be exposed. We disagreed. One cannot be that optimistic in today's world.

In the world of journalism, we often believe that in the present times, an optimist is one who believes things can only get worse from what they are now and a pessimist is one who believes they cannot get any more worse than what they already are.

Nothing comes easy in life. We recommended Mushrif take the legal route. A public interest litigation (PIL) filed in the high court could pave the way to justice.

Mushrif had to undergo so much humiliation, despite the fact that his brother Hasan Mushrif was not only a Nationalist Congress Party (NCP) leader, but also a minister in the Congress–NCP coalition-run state government in power. He had raised his voice, but could not gather enough support to sustain.

Mushrif slowly began to open up to us. We asked him for a formal interview but he categorically refused. He said that would not be appropriate as the investigation report was still under wraps. We cajoled him to brief us on the proceedings undertaken in the stamp scam so far, but he did not concede to our request. He tried to wrap up the meeting by citing that he was getting late for a court case. Another case related to the matter was listed in the courts. He needed to attend the hearing. We took a chance and asked him to brief us on the matter, to which he agreed.

We stepped out of Mushrif's house and within one and a half hours, reached Pune civil sessions court. When Mushrif arrived there, the cameraman took his visuals.

I had gone with my cameraman, but Mandar had come alone. He had locally arranged for a video camera.

Mushrif stepped out of the court and we started asking him questions on camera. There were questions about the present case, though we had not an iota of interest in it. After two or three questions, Mandar came straight to the point. 'Mushrif sir, you have made certain accusations regarding the Telgi stamp scam. What are those accusations?'

Mushrif was a bit startled. We had asked the question and broken our promise to him. This had become a baiting technique in TV journalism and we were mere by-products of that contrived system. The camera was on. Mushrif couldn't curse us despite his will to do so. He stayed quiet with deep anguish on his face.

'Mushrif sir, you are a high-ranking police officer. It is a matter of grave concern and the common public's interests are directly aligned to this matter. Despite knowing this, you are still maintaining a stoic silence. You can at least share what transpired in the case? Your loyalties must bend towards the common man.' I disguised with idealism my promise-breaking narrative and finally succeeded.

Mushrif ultimately broke his silence and gave a terse reply. 'There were irregularities in work done by my subordinate officers and their conduct was suspicious. I conveyed my observations to my senior officers in this matter.'

And with this, we had hit the goldmine. Mushrif left the court, disgruntled and upset at the whole dramatic shift.

And we gave solace to each other, saying when things don't work your way, you have to make them work for you.

Mandar and I had lunch together after Mushrif left. We knew each other's motive to be in Pune by now. We both lied to each other during further discussions. Despite having a copy of the investigation report, I lied to Mandar and told him I was trying to get hold of the report. Mandar, on the contrary, said he had the report and would soon be doing a reportage on the case on TV.

Both of us tried and failed miserably at hiding our true intent and emotions related to the case. We were both sceptical, so there was no room for argument. Mandar left for Mumbai after lunch.

The TV news would have been futile without any video clips on Telgi. Thus, we needed to shoot videos of Telgi. Cameraman Rokde shared that Pune's Dinmaan cable news had video footage of Telgi. Fortunately for us, Rokde had connections there, so he left to organize for the clips.

I was quite stressed and so, instead of accompanying Rokde to get the footage, I opted to stay back at the hotel. Mandar's statement that he had a copy of the report had dampened my spirits. We left for Mumbai post Rokde's return with the Telgi case-related video footage. I arrived in Mumbai, heartbroken.

9

Waiting for the Day to End

10–13 April 2003

Thursday to Sunday

The fact that Mandar had a copy of the report was playing havoc on my mind. I started working half-heartedly and felt so dejected that I skipped work the next day (10 April). The whole day I spent introspecting, reflecting, ruminating, distressing and yet staying hopeful. I met my 'source' who had given me the report. I asked him if he had shared the report with someone else as well. He refused, but also said that he had given me the report before it was officially submitted. Now that it had been submitted, it would pass through many tables in the DGP's office and the ministry. There was a probability of it being outed by someone else. The excerpts might find a way out, if not the report in its entirety. He understood my disappointment but suggested that I continue with my investigative work. He believed there were only a few reporters who could carry this report to its final conclusion.

I felt mentally agile the next day (11 April), and opened the newspapers with the apprehension of finding this news in between the folds of some newspaper. I heaved a sigh of relief. This process continued for the next four days. Somehow, I reached the office. I had to finish some pending shooting work and then begin the report.

While I was still at the office, Jitendra Dixit of Star News called me. After exchanging greetings, he asked if I was working on any special story. I denied. He let it go, but after some time, asked the same question. I again lied to him. But his inquisitiveness set alarm bells ringing in my head.

I chanced upon Neha Purav of In Mumbai News during the afternoon shoot. Over a cup of tea, she asked me if I was working on an exclusive story. She said the NDTV News List had an exclusive story written in front of my name. The whole matter was clear to me now. Our office had initiated a new routine of emailing a list of daily news listings, along with the names of the news reporters preparing the news. It was quite possible that a colleague at NDTV may have mentioned it in passing to another journalist, and the word had gone out to the fraternity. Some news reporters had a habit of keeping tabs on other channels through moles within the system. It had become an accredited practice in TV journalism owing to the cutthroat competition and people were ever ready to jump over others' heads to get ahead and stake their claims to glory. To have too much fame and success to enjoy, too soon and in too little time. Some reporters were pros at this stilted game and would not hesitate to use all the dirty tricks of the trade, from cajoling to bribing, to justify the means to the end. Their insecurities drove them to devise deceptive means to reveal others' secrets. Some had gained name and fame in journalism just by resorting to these nefarious ways.

It was a wise decision to not trust anyone at the Mumbai office with my secret. I resolved to maintain secrecy as much as I could. I didn't want to risk anything until our channel went live. My absence was felt within the journalist tribe and the market was abound with rumours that I was silently working on an exclusive.

The next day was Saturday (12 April)—just two more days to the channel's launch. Half of the shooting was still left. I still had to script it and get it edited. I was determined to edit my report only one day in advance, that is, on Sunday, to maintain total secrecy.

I went to a cybercafe to draft my script, and avoided writing it in the office amidst the hullabaloo and commotion. Then, post lunch, I shared the news with my local editors, Srinivas Jain and Abhigyan Prakash. I also showed them the Jaiswal Report and explained the whole scenario. Both praised my work. I requested them not to discuss the matter with anyone. Srinivas did not take my request kindly. The rest of the day was spent shooting.

The next day (April 13), my worst fears came alive. Our news list declared that I was working on an exclusive report related to the Telgi stamp scam. My reporter colleagues who were already suspecting that I was working on an exclusive, started making persistent inquiries. I averted the discussion each time and did not divulge any details. Not that I distrusted my colleagues, but this was my style of working. And I knew no one would have believed me then had I told them this was the biggest scam our country had ever witnessed and that NDTV's name would always be associated with its exposure.

I edited my news story that day. Editing is a crucial element in TV journalism. A cameraman and a video editor share equal responsibility in this process of refining a news report. Behind one person visible on the TV screen are twenty pillars of strength working behind the camera, making sure that news goes out perfectly. A TV presenter earns name and fame by his screen presence but the ones behind the scene continue to work without getting much credit.

I edited my report with my old and trustworthy editor, Faiyaz Dalvi. Faiyaz has a unique flair for editing and transforming an ordinary-looking report into a charismatic blockbuster. We finished the editing work in six hours.

The channel's 'dry run' began at night. A dry run is like a last rehearsal. The pre-live stage which ascertains the good and bad of the telecast lineup. It helps to make the necessary changes in advance. The dry run was successful. The others at the office watched my story for the first time. Almost all of the Mumbai office was present there. Everyone appreciated me. The secret was out in the open now. I was hoping that since no reporter had come close to this story until now, nothing could be done in the next sixteen hours. However, a sword named Mandar Parab still hung above my head.

A controversy and the associated danger aside, Parab was the last man standing between me and my destiny. That night before the channel launch, I spent oscillating between hope and ambition.

10
The Bullet Has Left the Barrel

14 April 2003

Monday

Finally, D-day was here. Our channel was scheduled to launch at 2 p.m. This was my penultimate day of challenge. I got up in the morning and switched on Sahara News. There was no reference made to the stamp scam anywhere.

I purchased all the newspapers printed in Mumbai and scanned them. No news on Telgi on any of the pages. I exhaled a breath of relief.

Before leaving for the office, I instructed my wife to keep a close eye on Sahara News and in case any report broke on the Jaiswal Report, she was to inform me immediately.

It was decided that Srinivas Jain would interview R.S. Sharma in English and Abhigyan Prakash in Hindi. I reached there out of curiosity. I wanted to observe what R.S. Sharma's reactions would be. What kind of facial expressions would he wear? It was a subject of academic interest for me.

The scheduled time was 10 a.m. but Sharma did not reach his office even by 11 a.m. His staff informed us that he wasn't expected in the office until that evening.

Since the Delhi office had given clear instructions not to air the report without R.S. Sharma's reactions, Srinivas Jain and Abhigyan Prakash, too, had started getting anxious as they were the anchors of the news programme and this exclusive interview was critical for their show.

Ultimately, I called R.S. Sharma. He said he could not make it to the interview. I handed the phone to Srinivas Jain. Jain spoke to Sharma. Jain said he would be highly grateful if Sharma could make it to his office by 11.30 a.m. As planned earlier, he was told, it would be a routine interview. Since NDTV was starting their own channel, they wanted to interview him regarding the growing footprint of the underworld in Mumbai. The idea was to catch him off guard during the interview, and abruptly question him about the Jaiswal Report on the Telgi scam. We knew very well that had we informed Sharma about our real motive behind interviewing him, he would have never agreed to come.

Finally, the interview commenced. Abhigyan opened the conversation with an easy question on the Mumbai underworld and the actions taken so far by Mumbai Police to curb the underworld presence in the city. This was a good warmup exercise to settle the interviewee and put him at ease. After finishing the formality of three or four normal questions, Abhigyan raised the ultimate question.

'Sharma ji, while you were Pune's police commissioner, there was an investigation report submitted regarding the suspicious role played by many police personnel in the Telgi stamp scam. It includes some citations against you.'

Sharma's face went ashen. The bullet had hit the target. Stress lines appeared on his forehead. Getting no response from Sharma, Abhigyan Prakash asked again, 'What do you have to say about the observations made about you in that report?'

'I know nothing about that report,' Sharma said feebly, crestfallen.

Abhigyan fired the missile that had been saved until now for closure. 'The report says that you were responsible for various acts of omission and commission. It recommends that the government must take action against you. You also tried to shield the accused corrupt officers, and you were a bad influence on the case.'

Sharma was in shock. He had probably realized by now that we were in possession of the Jaiswal Report. That's why our questions were based on the essence of the report.

He responded carefully, 'I do not know. I haven't seen the report yet.'

Abhigyan continued his line of firing.

'We have access to that report and it clearly declares you guilty,' Abhigyan said, dramatically waving a bunch of loose sheets in the air.

'I have no clue which report you are referring to.'

'You are the police commissioner of Mumbai and not of Ghaziabad or Gazipur. This is why we are asking you again and again. The nation wants to know what exactly happened.' This was Abhigyan's redeeming quality. He had a unique way of questioning and seizing his target in a strong grip. I may not have been personally fond of Abhigyan, but I couldn't negate his quality of interrogation.

'I told you I haven't seen the report. How can I give my reaction to it?' Sharma's tone was turning ice cold. The next two or three questions and answers were almost an action replay of the above. Finally, the interview came to an end, and the departure ritual started. Abhigyan tried to sweet-talk Sharma and bandage his wounds. This is common in journalism and often happens behind the camera. During the casual discussion, Abhigyan told Sharma that I had procured the report, and had been working on it for the last few days. He praised my investigative journalism ethic in front of Sharma. On his way out, Sharma glanced at him and smiled. I also bid him goodbye but somehow I had an inkling that Sharma had caught a whiff. I was well aware of the demeanour of police personnel. Sharp mind, calm nature, ever-smiling and innocent face, always friendly with journalists. I had known R.S. Sharma for the past six years and he was always friendly towards me. But things were going to change from today. Sharma's eyes spoke volumes and signalled a change of attitude towards me in the future.

We left the police commissioner's office around 12.30 p.m. Abhigyan, Srinivas and I left separately. This conveys the relationship we shared. I called my wife immediately after leaving the police commissioner's office and asked her if Sahara News had aired the Telgi scam news yet. I let out a deep breath when her response was a clear 'No'.

About the same time, at around 12.45 p.m., our political correspondent Sameeran Walvekar was covering a programme being organized at Worli's Nehru Centre. He took Maharashtra's home minister Chhagan Bhujbal's reaction on the Telgi matter and Bhujbal gave a non-confirmatory answer. He congratulated himself for a monumental scam being exposed during his tenure. He said he hadn't seen the report yet and appropriate actions would be taken after the report had been reviewed.

All facets of the report were now complete. Mushrif, R.S. Sharma, Bhujbal—all sides had been interviewed. In journalism jargon, the report was 'balanced' in all aspects. I was waiting for the clock to strike two with bated breath. On my way, I purchased all the afternoon newspapers such as *Mid Day*, *Afternoon*, *Mahanagar* and *Dopahar Ka Saamna*. I skimmed through all of them, but found no mention of the Telgi scam anywhere. I felt relieved. I was the last mile away from my destination, yet my patience knew no bounds.

There was still the one possible roadblock that could keep my news from turning into a historical news. Mandar Parab and his Sahara News channel. Exactly at 12.55 p.m., I called home and asked my wife to leave everything and sit glued to Sahara News for the next two hours. Every minute of this last one hour was like many hours for me. As per the programme schedule, when the channel was launched at 2 p.m., my news report would be the first to be aired. Post that, there would be a live interview with me on 'OB', or an Outdoor Broadcast, that is, from a van equipped for live telecast outside the office. At exactly 2 p.m., I stationed myself on our building's terrace. I was supposed to talk to the news broadcaster via the camera installed there. I called home every ten minutes between 1 p.m. and 2 p.m. to check if Sahara News had aired Telgi scam news, but the answer was negative each time.

Exactly at 2 p.m., the channel was launched. I was on the terrace. There were earpieces in my ears and I could hear voices through them. An earpiece is a small instrument that can be attached to the ear, which connected us to the voice of a news broadcaster sitting in Delhi. We can communicate with them via the earpiece and the camera installed at our end.

NDTV began its first broadcast precisely at 2 p.m. I heard the voice of 'NDTV India' channel's news anchor Dibang in my earpiece. He introduced the channel, telling the story behind the formation and structure of both the channels. Then he began introducing my report. He said this was NDTV's first official news, and its first exclusive

The Bullet Has Left the Barrel

reporting. Then he showed my report. Once the report was over, Dibang said, 'Let's move to Mumbai now and talk to our correspondent Sanjay Singh, who was instrumental in getting this confidential report to you.'

Then, a question-and-answer session followed between Dibang and me. Amongst my answers was my reaction to the lacklustre attitude shown by the state home minister Chhagan Bhujbal in this whole affair.

As I reached the office, everyone welcomed me with a big round of applause. A cake was brought to celebrate the successful launch of the channel. I was asked to cut the cake, despite so many senior journalists being around. After the cake cutting, a round of champagne followed and the celebratory mode was turned on.

The first one to congratulate me on my report was Mandar Parab. When he called to congratulate me, I asked him if he had played the report on his channel, to which his response was 'No'. Then I started getting calls from everywhere, but mostly from policemen and media people. Everyone congratulated me on the sensational report. From these calls, I figured out that the report had wreaked havoc through the ranks of Mumbai Police. R.S. Sharma camp police personnel were down in the dumps. It was the same scenario with some confidants of Chhagan Bhujbal. I thought to myself: 'This was just the curtain raiser. The show is yet to begin.'

At night, I got to know from the office of *Indian Express* that they were printing the Jaiswal Report in the next morning's edition. I asked my resident editor Srinivas Jain about it, and he said that he had given the report to *Indian Express*. I took great offence to this—I should have been consulted before sharing the report. After all, it was a result of my blood, toil, tears and sweat. Informing Jain that I would be sharing it with other newspapers as well, I stepped out of his office. The same night, I shared the report with newspapers like *Mahanagar* and *Navbharat Times*. I asked *Times of India* too, but their reporter didn't sound too interested.

Drunk on my success after a euphoric day filled with a tremendous sense of achievement, I completely forgot how tough the same day would have been for Mandar. I had gone through days of trials and tribulations until the moment the report was telecast, and my worst fears were Mandar's reality right now.

Mandar had submitted the file at Sahara News before me, but somehow, it wasn't telecast in time. There could not be a more sinister irony than this for a journalist. I could completely empathize with Mandar. All his efforts had been futile. He was ahead of me and won the race too, but still did not get the winner's trophy.

The fame and accolades coming my way would have been his had Sahara News telecast the news before us. Time had played a cruel game with him. He may not have expressed his anguish but I could completely relate to his inner turmoil, as I had also been fighting against that uncertainty like him, until a few hours back.

11

Debauchery in Custody

15 April 2003

Tuesday

The newspapers were raving about my report. I reached the office early in the morning and filed my second report. Whereas the first report only exposed the role of R.S. Sharma in the corruption, the second report had a summary of allegations against all eight corrupt police officers listed together. This was again an exclusive report.

The same day, R.S. Sharma invited all crime reporters of Mumbai newspapers, and gave off-the-record clarifications on all matters published so far. Sharma told the journalists this was scandal-mongering by those who had lost the race to him to become Mumbai's police commissioner. The arrow pointed towards Thane's commissioner

S.M. Shangari. No TV reporter was called inside. NDTV reporter Sameeran Walvekar was treated abominably, being made to sit outside Sharma's office and not granted an interview either until the end.

I received another report by Subodh Jaiswal through a 'source' on the same day. Written on 10 January, this report too was sensational in its own way.

In October 2002, Mumbai Police had arrested Telgi in a murder case. But despite being in police custody for eighty-five days, Telgi was not put in the police lockup for even a single day. He was made to stay either at his Cuffe Parade residence, his Colaba flat or at Sion's Hotel Ashray and provided all kinds of comforts in police custody. But this game ended on 9 January 2003, when the Maharashtra SIT and Karnataka SIT raided Telgi's Cuffe Parade house under a joint operation. This raid was supervised by Maharashtra SIT Chief DIG Subodh Jaiswal and Karnataka SIT Chief Additional DGP R. Sri Kumar.

They were amazed at the scene they witnessed there. The house that Pune Police had allegedly sealed was open, with the seal broken. Inside, Telgi was comfortably at home, having tea and biscuits. Two police constables were seen enjoying food made by Telgi's servants and the third constable was fast asleep in the adjacent room. Assistant Inspector Dilip Kamath, who was in-charge of the investigation, was missing from there. Jaiswal declared Mumbai Police's clarification of calling this a ploy to trap a warranted criminal baseless and dubious.

Debauchery in Custody

Jaiswal sent his report dated 10 January 2003 to Ashok Basak, additional chief secretary (home). In his report, Jaiswal described the scene:

> On 09/01/2003 Jaiswal along with R. Sri Kumar (Addl DGP, Karnataka and head of Karnataka SIT) and few other members of SIT visited various spots in Mumbai where seizures of Telgi's fake stamps have taken place. After visiting Dana Bandar and Carnac Bandar areas, the team left for visiting spots in Cuffe Parade and Colaba areas.
>
> They reached 7, Cuffe Parade. 7, Cuffe Parade is a flat where seizures had taken place earlier in the Pune case. At 4.45 p.m. on 09/01/2003 SIT rang the doorbell. There was delay in opening the entrance door of the flat. The door was opened by a person in civvies who was later identified as a police constable of Mumbai Crime Branch. Two more police constables were present in the flat out of which one was sleeping in adjacent room. All three policemen were in plainclothes.
>
> On entering the flat, SIT found signs of regular habitation in flat and Telgi was also present in flat. Telgi was sitting comfortably in his office room enjoying tea–biscuits.
>
> Inside the house, personal garments of Telgi were neatly laid and the bed showed signs of regular usage. A bag belonging to Telgi consisting of his

medicines and some clothes was also found on the table.

Inside the flat, there were two young boys one of whom was busy cooking in the kitchen while the other was looking after the household.

There was absolutely no doubt that Telgi had been conscientiously taken to the flat to enjoy the luxurious normal life while still in the police custody with full connivance of police personnel, instead of being in the police lock-up.

On questioning, it was revealed that they had come to the spot along with police officer Dilip Kamath of Crime Branch who was incidentally not present in the flat. On further questioning, the constables replied that they were waiting in a trap laid to arrest suspected accused Tabrej.

According to Jaiswal, in this report, the alleged raison d'être for the physical presence of Telgi in his own flat while being in police custody, which was made out by the police personnel of waiting in a trap, does not hold water for the following reasons:

- If it was a trap, then one policeman wouldn't have been sleeping the way he was.
- In-charge of the team, Assistant Inspector Dilip Kamath should have been present to spring the trap, if at all the reason was true. Intriguingly, his physical

absence from the scene totally falsifies the assertions of the police personnel about the actual cause of their presence.

- The presence of Telgi's clothes bag at the flat belies any reason whatsoever that any such trap had actually been planned.

- It is obviously foolish to expect the absconding Tabrej to show up at a flat to meet the arrested Telgi or anybody else, unless it was being planned to arrange a clandestine meeting between Telgi, his lawyer and the other accomplice, with full and clear complicity of the Mumbai Crime Branch policemen.

- If it was a trap, then the door should have been opened immediately since they had been anticipating the arrival of the absconding accused. This was not done.

- No physical measures were put into place to prevent an escape attempt by Telgi.

- The overall state of 'relaxed inaction' and 'air of levity' in the flat precludes any possibility of a police trap being put in place.

- The presence of two servants in the flat also makes the 'trap story' totally improbable and impossible.

Jaiswal went on to write,

> I would like to place on record that DCP Pradeep Sawant had been warned telephonically on

3 January 2003 that Telgi had been granted all creature comforts while in police custody by Crime Branch officers. Specifically, I had mentioned that Telgi, while in police custody, had been taken to Alankar Lodge by Crime Branch officers where he had collected monthly earnings of the lodge. DCP Sawant had assured me that he would look into the above facts and take counter measures to prevent such acts. Obviously this has not happened.

The report also stated that investigation of cases registered against Telgi in Mumbai had been carried out in a shoddy manner. In one case, he was not arrested even after his anticipatory bail had been rejected. He clearly mentioned that 'facts establish the perverse conduct of the Crime Branch police personnel in the instant case beyond doubt' and further, the report also forewarned that 'the Crime Branch officials will attempt to fudge the lock-up registers, case diaries and even make an arrest in order to justify their unauthorized and illegal presence in the flat.'

Jaiswal also pointed out a few interesting points, as follows:

- Telgi was not making concerted efforts to seek bail and neither had his lawyers been opposing police custody effectively.
- It follows quite logically that it was comfortable for Telgi to be in police custody and simultaneously carry out activities through his illegal crime syndicate while in police custody.

- The main area of operation of Telgi's crime syndicate was Mumbai and his continued presence there was to obviously dispose of/relocate his operations.
- This case proved beyond doubt the presence of Telgi in his own flat while in Mumbai Police custody which had been locked up by Pune Police.

The report also made two important recommendations that Assistant Inspector Dilip Kamath, who allegedly laid the so-called trap along with three other policemen, should be dismissed under Section 311(2)(B) of the Constitution in order to send a strong message to other police personnel involved in perverse conduct. Strict actions should be taken against the investigative officer and supervisory officers who were monitoring the day-to-day investigations against Telgi.

Subodh Jaiswal wrote this report exactly one day after the incident, that is, on 10 January, and sent it to Maharashtra's additional chief secretary (home).

This was also shared with the police commissioner of Mumbai, R.S. Sharma. Based on the Jaiswal Report recommendations, Mumbai Police immediately suspended Assistant Inspector Dilip Kamath and the other three policemen. DCP Pradeep Sawant was asked to carry out the departmental inquiry but when his name sprang up in the case, the investigation was moved under DCP Ankush Shinde.

12

An Encounter with Pradeep Sawant

Pradeep Sawant was the biggest target of Jaiswal's report. He was counted as the sharpest one amidst his peers at the Mumbai Crime Branch division. He had started an encounter drive against organized underworld syndicates during his three years' tenure at the Crime Branch, come down hard on organized gangs and incapacitated them. And he was particularly biased towards one faction in the Crime Branch: Inspector Pradeep Sharma and Daya Nayak's faction. These people ran a parallel Crime Branch, in a way. Sawant and his faction was considered a powerful and high-profile group.

Sawant's office was the first one I called after receiving the latest report. I got to know that he was on leave and would be back the next day. The report had made adverse comments about Sawant. Thus, taking down his reaction

An Encounter with Pradeep Sawant

was important. I dialled Sawant's mobile phone. We knew each other well. After exchanging pleasantries, I told him I had the latest report and was seeking his reaction on it.

After a brief pause, Sawant asked, 'Where did you get the copy of the report from?'

It was a foolish question. No journalist would ever betray his 'source'. I again asked him for his reaction.

Sawant responded, 'My friend, please check once. It is a secret report and action can be taken for breach of the Official Secrets Act.'

'It doesn't matter. Just share your reactions,' I said, throwing caution to the winds.

'No ... you should also consult your legal department. Otherwise it may lead to legal action later.' Sawant tried to scare me off, but I could sense fear emanating from his voice.

I figured that he would not relent from his stand, so I resorted to Formula 44 of journalism.

'I already have it vetted by our legal department and we have also reviewed the Press Council of India norms. Everything is in order. The chairman of the press council is a retired judge,' I lied.

Sawant remained silent on the other end. My trick had worked. When I asked him for his reaction again, he said, 'You can quote that since this is a secret report, I cannot comment on it in any manner.'

I knew he was trying to get rid of me. I said, 'This report is scheduled for telecasting on TV tomorrow, that is 16 April. If you feel up to it, you can call me any time to give your reaction.' Our call came to a close at this point.

I got busy preparing my report that was to be telecast the next day. At night, I received a call from the chief editor of NDTV, Rajdeep Sardesai.

'Sanjay, I just got a call from Chhagan Bhujbal. He was saying that Pradeep Sawant was his best officer, and Sanjay is after him. So much has already been done against R.S. Sharma, why target Sawant now?'

I responded, 'I really can't go about shielding Bhujbal's near and dear ones. I have filed a news story on the basis of Jaiswal's report which has comments against Sawant.'

'Very good! Just remember whatever the news may be, we must have corresponding proof of the same with us, otherwise Sawant and his troop will come after you,' Rajdeep said. 'You are doing good work. Keep it up. The story will go as is.'

One thing was certain. Sawant must have informed Bhujbal that I was working on a report against him. I was amazed at the close proximity between the two. What was it actually that compelled the state home minister and deputy chief minister Chhagan Bhujbal to make that call for DCP Sawant? There were many DCP rank officials like him all over Maharashtra.

Sawant had also fired a big shot. Instead of approaching a senior police official like the joint commissioner or the DGP, he had got the home minister to pursue his case. This was truly strange.

I knew that in the present political scenario, police officers approached politicians instead of their superiors, in case of need. For the past few years, from transfers, postings to any other recommendations, police officials from constables to the police commissioner were seen bowing before their political masters. Nowadays, the home ministry also feels more like a police post than a functioning ministry.

There is a fixed rate for each post. Mumbai is considered the most lucrative posting. From DCP to constable, all sorts of connections are used by officers to land the most lucrative postings or police stations. Hotel owners, builders, businessmen become their financiers. It has all become a business now. Investments are made and then recoveries are made, along with interest. It is dangerous to watch these transactions become part of street gossip. Not that all police officers are corrupt, but such personnel manage to bag one or two prominent postings. Most of the clean-image officials are given administrative posts. The ones who refuse to compromise on their values and refrain from boot-licking of politicians are given less important postings. Seniority and competence finds no place in the system. The one who finds an equilibrium amidst this commotion survives and prospers.

All of us journalists covering the crime beat were very well versed with this. Some stayed quiet to get the news and some collaborated with them. And the ones who did not fall under either of the categories ended up spending a life in anonymity. Such wrongdoing was rampant in the Mumbai crime branch and the DCP was Pradeep Sawant. I filed my report, which was scheduled for telecast the next morning, that is, Wednesday, 16 April. Reaching home late, I was wondering what would be the reaction of Bhujbal and Sawant upon watching the report in the news the next day. They must have assumed that they had managed to put a stop to the news. Though one nagging doubt was still troubling my mind. My new report wasn't exclusive any more as both Bhujbal and Sawant knew of the 10 January Jaiswal Report. They both shared close proximity with many journalists and were bound to have known about it. I fell asleep while attempting to untangle my jumbled-up thoughts.

13

Damage Control and More Damage

16 April 2003

Wednesday

The news was telecast on NDTV at 7 a.m. the next morning. Within an hour, Sahara and Zee News telecast the same news. I thought of an old adage in the case of Sawant. *'Chaubey ji gaye the Chhabbey ji banne, magar Dubey ji ban kar lautey.'* This means 'when a person acts overly smart, he ends up falling flat on his face'. As efforts were being made to curtail news broadcasting on one channel, it was perhaps too late as three other news channels were already running the story.

Bemused at his pitiful condition, I was getting ready to go to the office when my mobile rang. It was Sachin Vaze, a sub-inspector at Mumbai crime branch. He thought too much of himself. A computer specialist and a part of Senior Inspector Pradeep Sharma's squad, he had been with Mumbai crime branch for years. I had already suspected the reason for his call but I feigned ignorance and continued to talk. After exchanging pleasantries, Sachin Vaze asked, 'So, how is work?'

My response was 'All right'. Nothing special.'

He asked, 'And the channel has been launched?'

Despite being immersed in the mayhem the NDTV report had created within the police department, he had asked me this question. So-called 'smart' people have their own ways of inquiring. It is best to play a fool in front of them. In Mumbaiya language, it is called '*yeda banke peda khana*', which means that 'a fool flatters himself, a wise man flatters the fool'. I also resolved to let him come to the point, and not blow my own trumpet on the roaring success of my report.

'Yes, it has been launched. Did you watch it?'

'It was launched with great pomp and show,' Sachin informed.

'Thank you,' I said.

Vaze asked, 'Did you show the news about DCP Sawant?'

I had begun to enjoy this game, so I lied. 'I had filed the report last night, not sure if it has been telecast yet.' I knew he was about to lose patience any minute now.

'It has been telecast,' he said.

I asked, 'How did you find the report?' I was also determined not to let go so easily.

Instead of responding, he made a statement. 'Do damage control now.'

Now he was in the open field. He was acting as the guardian angel for Pradeep Sawant. He himself was still entangled as a suspect in the alleged murder case of an accused in the Ghatkopar bomb blast, and here he was trying to bail out Sawant.

I asked naively, 'Damage control! How? The story will not stop, whatever may happen.'

My response was unanticipated. After a pause, he spoke. 'At least interview DCP Sawant sir.'

I said, 'I will certainly do that. You speak to Sawant. We at NDTV broadcast balanced news, giving opportunity to all sides, taking views and counterviews of the involved. That is why I asked Sawant for his reactions yesterday, but he refused to comment. Why don't you ask him? He listens to you since you are close to him.'

'All right. I will try to persuade DCP sir for the interview. What time will you come?' he responded.

'1 p.m. should be fine,' I said.

'I will inform other TV channels too.' Sensing my indifference, he threw a bait.

I confirmed the time and disconnected.

The police had their own propaganda mechanism. Sachin Vaze had all the qualities of a good media manager. This is an individual flair, as no police academy teaches this skill, nor is it part of the duty of a suspended police officer.

(A few years later, Sachin Vaze, who was destined to earn infamy, was accused and jailed for planting explosives outside Ambani's house and covering the heinous act with the murder of one of his own friends. The mention here is to prove the adage 'coming events cast their shadows before'.)

I was amazed at what a blind follower of Sawant's Sachin Vaze was. At 1 p.m. sharp, I was at the press conference room on the premises of the Mumbai police commissioner's office. The press room was made by the police for the convenience of the press. All the journalists covering the crime beat gathered together here. The press room was quite crowded. Journalists from ten to twelve TV channels and the same number from print newspapers were present there. This was the magic of Sachin Vaze. Pradeep Sawant made an appearance after some time. He said he wanted to talk 'off the record'.

'Off the record' in journalism meant the statement would not be made on camera, and the corresponding news could not be printed in the name of the person sharing the information. After all cameras were removed, he shared his views. Later, when the TV journalists insisted on a statement, Sawant left, saying that he would try to get a statement from his senior and head of crime branch, Joint Police Commissioner Satyapal Singh. After some time, we got a call from the joint police commissioner's office to

Damage Control and More Damage

meet him. Satyapal Singh had been newly appointed and the report flashed against Sawant was based on the scandal that had happened during his predecessor joint police commissioner Sridhar Wagal's tenure.

In this sense, Satyapal Singh's hands were clean in this matter, and he was giving a statement out of his moral duty as the head of the crime branch. Satyapal Singh's command on ethical codes and explaining matters is unparalleled. He put forward his reaction on the matter in a way that the journalists could not nail him. For every question, his response was that the work at the crime branch was highly classified, and based on the recommendations of the SIT report, four policemen had already been suspended. DCP Ankush Shinde was conducting internal investigations on the matter. He had sidelined the question on the concluding date for the ongoing investigation for the last four months. Then, Mandar Parab raised a question.

Even Mandar didn't know the repercussions of his question. He asked, 'Mr Satyapal Singh, do all the statements you have given today imply that you are trying to shield Sawant?'

Satyapal Singh jolted, then regained his composure and responded. 'There is nothing like that. I am stating things as a matter of fact. These incidents did not happen during my tenure as the chief of the crime branch.'

Like a seasoned senior police official, Satyapal Singh ended up saying a lot without saying anything. He did not commit to anything. I caught a glimpse of mischief in Mandar's glinting eyes. Usually, when a journalist has a premonition about a news, he emanates such radiance.

After Satyapal Singh stepped out, Mandar called out Sawant from the midst of journalists leaving the room.

'This interview was futile. Satyapal neither defended you, nor said anything in your favour.'

Sawant looked troubled. He asked for Mandar's suggestion on the next course of action. Mandar advised him to present his own point of view. Sawant agreed. After some time, Sawant appeared for the TV interview. All cameras were in position. I also asked a question and Sawant dug his own grave with the last line of his answer. That was the line that would be used in the SIT court trial against him.

Sawant said, 'The report you are referring to is a secret report. It will be inappropriate to comment on it, as the investigations are ongoing in this matter.' And then Sawant said the grave-digging line, 'But this must not be forgotten that the 830 crore rupees worth of fake stamps recovered from Bhiwandi were only because of the trap we laid at Telgi's house.'

Many questions followed this but the result was zero. We came back to the office after the interview and added Sawant's reaction to the final news edit before airing it.

But there was one thing that continued to trouble me. In response to my question, Sawant could have just responded with 'I cannot comment on the secret report', which he did state, but why did he add the bit about the raid? My question had not been about the raid at all. Why did he say something so disastrous that became the reason for his arrest later? It constituted evidence against him. I didn't know what time it was when Sawant's own judgement failed him. Somehow, I cannot recollect the relevant Sanskrit quote from holy scriptures which means 'often all the powers of your mind fail you when you need them the most, that is in the wake of an impending disaster'.

14
Heat Rising

17–23 April 2003

Thursday to Wednesday

Way to Thane

Next day, I got the information that the police had captured two terrorists of the Lashkar-e-Taiba in Thane, a city adjacent to Mumbai. I stepped out to cover this news. DCP Pradeep Sawant called me in the afternoon. There were only a handful of occasions when Sawant had called me directly. I appreciated him skipping the step of having a mediator like Sachin Vaze calling to connect with me. After exchanging greetings, he asked, 'What is your plan for the day?'

'Headed towards Thane to cover another news. I am not able to do any further stories on the Telgi scam,' I responded.

He asked his real question, 'Have you aired my interview which you took yesterday?'

'Telecast, yes,' I replied.

'It wasn't telecast. That is what my people told me,' Sawant said.

He must have been misinformed or whoever shared this with Sawant may have missed the 8 p.m. bulletin last night.

I clarified, 'We showed it at 8 p.m. and it played all night. You can counter-check once. If you wish, can I send over the recording to you to watch?'

'No. That won't be necessary.' Trusting my self-confidence in my response, he disconnected the phone.

I filed the Thane news that day.

A Round of Navi Mumbai

There was nothing special today. Deputy Chief Minister Chhagan Bhujbal was making an appearance at two programmes organized at Navi Mumbai, which is a little away from Mumbai. The state's highest ranked police official DGP Subash Malhotra was scheduled to attend one of the programmes. I also went there in the hope that Bhujbal may publicly say something about the Telgi scam at the function. But Bhujbal didn't say anything to that effect at the Navi Mumbai police commissioner's office, and left for the next programme in a rush. I took Malhotra's interview at the office. During the interview, Malhotra refused to make any comments on the Jaiswal Report. Malhotra said whichever official had leaked Jaiswal's report to NDTV had violated the police service conduct rules.

After the interview, during an informal discussion, he told me in English, 'You cooperate please and let us figure out the source of the leak. We can together single out the betrayer hiding within the system.'

I retorted in English, 'Malhotra sir, why don't you cooperate with us instead? We can reveal the traitors hiding within the system. The rotten ones who are tarnishing the police force's image and reputation. We will expose them together.'

Malhotra's displeasure at my response was evident, but he did not allow his feelings to reflect on his face. He was a veteran police professional. Someone who had spent decades in police service, he was a man of the world. The police commissioner of Navi Mumbai and Star News reporter Jitendra Dixit were also present during this conversation.

I was musing over the irony of the situation. Malhotra was silent on the misdeeds exposed in the Jaiswal Report, but he was insisting upon finding out how the report was leaked. Why was making the report public ethically wrong, and finding the source who leaked the report so important? What kind of police work was this? I remember the Tehelka tape case. All the people exposed in the case were reinstated in politics, and Tehelka had to face public criticism, followed by an inquiry against them.

All government agencies came down hard on Tehelka. The politicians vociferously criticized the practice of hidden camera recordings in the Tehelka case in TV debates. This is a sign of an incomplete and rotten democracy. I feel that the disjointed role of the fourth pillar of democracy also contributes to this commotion.

I got to know later that Malhotra gave out instructions to investigate the source of the report leak.

Outside his office, I met a freelance journalist, Prabhat. A freelancer is a journalist who does not work at one place, but sends his reports to different newspapers and if his news gets published, he gets paid for it. Prabhat, despite being a journalist, was so close to the policemen that some people considered him a part of the police force. He was considered especially close to DCP Pradeep Sawant. He had also accepted that publicly amongst many journalists. He initiated a conversation outside the office of the Navi Mumbai police commissioner.

'You have stirred up a hornet's nest!'

I replied, 'Yeah ... everyone's in the pits.'

'I also told those people, everyone else can be "managed", but Sanjay Singh is a tough cookie,' Prabhat said.

I felt the alleged 'those people' he was referring to were the corrupt officials of the police department involved in the case. After whiling away some time, he asked, 'Sanjay, why don't you seek police protection?'

'Police protection!' My head was spinning. 'What would I do with police protection? There is no threat to my life.'

But it was as if he was relaying a message. 'Keep it as a status symbol?'

I refused. 'What status symbol? I live in a 200 square foot one-room plus kitchen house and drive a fifteen-year-old motorcycle. I won't be able to afford it.'

Then Prabhat suggested a new solution. 'Do one thing. Get a licence for a revolver.'

'What would I do with a revolver? Who do I have to kill, and how would I manage the finances of one to two lakh rupees?' I responded.

'You take the licence now. Take the weapon later, if needed. I will manage everything. Everything remains within the family here.'

Prabhat's last statement made me start doubting his intentions.

I said, 'A licence without a weapon is redundant! I don't need either, as is. I am an able person and haven't done anything wrong. Then why create this facade?'

'You won't understand!' Prabhat finally surrendered.

He bid me adieu. I kept thinking about what he had said. Was this a kind of signal? Or was he my well-wisher, forewarning me of something untoward coming my way?

Keeping Prabhat's proximity with Pradeep Sawant in mind, I wondered if they were resorting to the age-old trick of advising or manipulating, bribing or harassing, and if nothing worked, then blackmail. Or was Prabhat trying to gain self-importance by unnecessarily interfering in a matter that was none of his business? There were a plethora of questions I wanted to ask and I could visualize some answers, too. But one thing was certain, I was becoming a thorn in the side of many in the police force. I left the police commissioner's office and within fifteen minutes, I was at Vishnudas Bhave Natyagruha, where Bhujbal's second appearance was scheduled. I stood waiting for Bhujbal at the gate. He came out after half an hour and gave an interview amidst his supporters.

After the interview was over, Bhujbal looked at me and said, smiling, 'Sanjay Singh, I understand NDTV had to launch a new channel, and they needed an inaugural sensational news to make an impact. You gave them that. The launch was fantastic. You have given sleepless nights to the police force. Now, please rest a bit and cool down.'

If Bhujbal hadn't spoken all these things in a lighter vein, I would have had enough reasons to look for the signs of threat in his words. I chose instead to respond with a smile and not say a thing. I reached the office and filed my story. The news story was about how on the one hand, the DGP and home minister created a hullabaloo over the leaking of the report, and on the other refused to comment on the recommendations it had made.

For me, this day was also quite significant and meaningful. There were varied signs that could be interpreted in many ways.

The third week of April proved disastrous for Mumbai Police but tremendously auspicious for me. My work found appreciation in the media circles. The Competitors bowed to my acumen, but it created a rift between Mandar and me. We kept this a secret from each other. I wondered if we had shown our loyalties towards our channels, instead of maintaining the essence of our friendship, or if there was stiff competition between us to hog all the fame. We continued to meet but maintained our distance as if we were strangers.

In the meanwhile, the crusade to give the whole issue a political hue began. Former chief minister and leader of the opposition from the Shiv Sena, Narayan Rane, started it. But he may also not have anticipated the quantum of effect his drive would have after eight months, that this matter would lead to the cornering of Bhujbal by the opposition parties, seeking his resignation.

In the future, Narayan Rane would switch loyalties to Congress, then move to Bharatiya Janata Party (BJP) and become a Central cabinet minister.

Rane, along with the delegates from opposition parties, Shiv Sena-BJP, met governor Mohammed Fazal and demanded the removal of Bhujbal from his post. BJP leaders Gopinath Munde and Nitin Gadkari were among the opposition parties' delegates.

Chhagan Bhujbal was no less. He struck back hard. Bhujbal too met with the governor and explained his situation. He also alleged that this scam had flourished between 1995 and 1998 and it was the Shiv Sena–BJP coalition government that had been in power back then. Bhujbal was right, in a way. But one salient point of democracy is that people, as well as journalists, who otherwise review all information with a fine-tooth comb, take allegations made by opposition parties rather lightly. Shiv Sena–BJP surrounded the ministry to protest. Bhujbal was a seasoned politician who managed to endure all the heat and dodge the bullet. The matter became so political that the battle turned into one between Bhujbal and the opposition. R.S. Sharma and other corrupt police personnel's roles were completely forgotten. Even other politicians preferred to observe quietly and refrain from commenting on the issue.

The interesting fact to observe was that while the Shiv Sena leader Narayan Rane was blowing up this issue, the print mouthpiece of his party *Saamna* was printing pro-R.S. Sharma news. Rane began to cut corners when confronted with a question about this. A case of one hand not knowing the tricks the other hand was pulling.

Have you not heard this dialogue in movies?

15

Clean Chit to Commissioner Sharma

24 April 2003

Thursday

DGP Subash Malhotra sent the Subodh Jaiswal Report to the government along with his comments on 23 April. Home Minister Chhagan Bhujbal called for a press conference at the ministry in haste on 24 April, and with his trademark flair, he spoke about giving a clean chit to R.S. Sharma and appropriate action against the other corrupt police officials.

- Investigation officers—Inspector Prakash Deshmukh and SP Mulani—were declared guilty in alignment with the recommendations made in the Jaiswal Report. Both were dismissed from service and orders were passed for internal inquiry to commence against them.
- Department inquiry orders passed against DCP Kishore Jadhav.
- Action to be taken against DCP Jai Jadhav and SP Ashok Kamble, but only after getting clarifications from them on the allegations made.
- Surprisingly, Additional Commissioner S.M. Mushrif also was hit in the process. Despite the allegations made by him being proven true, a departmental inquiry against him was ordered. Back then, many felt this to be too harsh a punishment for Mushrif.
- The statements made against R.S. Sharma were rather grave in nature. The recommendations given by Jaiswal on Sharma were acknowledged, but strangely, the government refused to take any action against Sharma. Out of nine accused officials, only Sharma was given a clean chit.
- The government had blindly followed the recommendations of DGP Malhotra. From his side, DGP Malhotra commented, 'As a Commissioner, R.S. Sharma was oblivious to the day-to-day activities

carried on in the investigation. Sharma cannot be held accountable for the act of omission and commission committed by officials working under him.'

The situation was such that the government did not even deem fit asking R.S. Sharma for an explanation. Some felt that this exclusion was an open statement to declare that 'this is our decision and you can do zilch about it'.

16

Shoot the Messenger: Pasricha Inquiry

May 2003

Sharma got a clean chit but it seems they were not done with me. The power and politics had to show their might somehow. It's human nature to want revenge. The inquiry for the report leak was initiated. To avoid any kind of controversy, an official with a non-partisan image, Maharashtra's additional DGP Parminder Singh Pasricha was asked to lead this inquiry. Pasricha was additional DGP (law and order) at that point of time. The eye on the gun was certainly DGP Malhotra's, I was the target and the gun was perched on the shoulder of Pasricha.

One fine evening, I got a call from Pasricha. I had known him for a long time. We used to meet occasionally when he was the joint commissioner of Mumbai, two years back. He maintained a casual approach during our conversations. This is why he inquired of my well-being first. Then he said, 'Sanjay, drop by my office for a cup of tea.'

Pasricha had a maverick approach. But I understood this was my call for roasting. I had been summoned for an inquiry. There was no point in dilly-dallying or offering any excuses, so I agreed.

Next day, I reached the head office of Maharashtra Police. Before leaving, I called up Mandar Parab and asked him to inform the media fraternity in case I got arrested. And if I did not step out within one hour, then the journalists must call Pasricha, though we both knew the scope of me getting arrested was very low.

Pasricha's office was right next to Malhotra's, on the first floor of the head office. I was called in after a wait of five minutes. Pasricha met me with a lot of warmth. We began our conversation with a dose of nostalgia and our old association. He praised my work in journalism. He then inquired after Mandar Parab. After our initial conversation, he put me at ease and I felt comfortable in the environment.

After some time, Pasricha came to the point.

'I have been asked to hold an inquiry,' sipping coffee, Pasricha mentioned gently. 'About the Jaiswal Report leak. It was a confidential report and it found its way to you.'

I cut him short and gave a resolute response. I had already thought about my line of response and decided offence would be the best defense in this situation. I said, 'This report was not with me alone. It was with many others. On 16 April 2003, Mumbai's joint commissioner Satyapal Singh waved a bundle of papers in front of dozens of journalists, and confirmed he had the report in his possession.' I was aware that the report had already reached many Indian Police Service (IPS) officers and the sole intention of this inquiry was to entrap me.

Pasricha said further, 'So shall we begin the inquiry?'

I nodded in agreement.

Pasricha asked me, 'Where did you get the Jaiswal Report from? Who leaked the report to you?'

I smiled. Pasricha was asking me the reason for my prosperity and the secret for my destruction.

I said, 'I cannot share. In journalism, we do not reveal the identity of our sources, not even to our superiors. Pasricha sir, you were the chief of the intelligence division, did you ever divulge details of your sources to anyone?'

And when I did not share the details of the original source of that report with my boss, closest friends and well-wishers, then why share with Pasricha? It would be a betrayal to my source and suicidal for me.

Pasricha said, 'I have to record something in the report. This answer of yours won't suffice.'

I thought that since he was so insistent, let me say something. I lied, 'See, our editor Rajdeep Sardesai gave me this report. Please record this as my official response in this matter.'

I knew no one was going to subject Rajdeep to an inquiry. These shenanigans and inquiries against me were child's play for DGP Malhotra, but he would think ten times before summoning Rajdeep for an inquiry.

'Where did Rajdeep get the report from?' Pasricha continued his line of questioning.

'We have some designated reporters to source such secret reports. One of them may have given it to Rajdeep. I neither know the identity, nor have their contact. It is all kept hidden from us.'

When you lie, you have to tell another lie to cover up the first one, then another and another, and the cycle goes on.

There was nothing more left to ask. Pasricha jotted down my answer. Both of us stayed silent for some time. Then, keeping the pen and paper aside, Pasricha broke the silence. 'Now tell me as a friend, buddy, where did you find the report?' Pasricha winked at me with his left eye. My eyes sparkled.

'DGP Malhotra gave me the report.' I shot the master stroke of lies. I knew Pasricha wouldn't ask me anything beyond that point. Worry lines appeared on Pasricha's forehead. He reciprocated my mischievous smile with a faint smile. There was nothing left to say and understand between us.

'I don't know what I said and don't know what you heard.'

After some small talk, I took his permission to leave. After meeting Pasricha, I realized that he was conducting his inquiry half-heartedly. This had forcefully been thrust on him and duty-bound by the discipline instilled in the police forces, he unwillingly conducted it. On the other side, Mandar had mischief. Pasricha had to explain to different journalists over the next half an hour that he had not arrested Sanjay Singh.

Though no one really knows what happened to that inquiry, the meeting with Pasricha gave me an insight into the police's mala fide intentions.

The same Pasricha later became DG of the Anti-Corruption Bureau, Police Commissioner of Mumbai, DGP of Maharashtra and, post-retirement, managed a prominent post at a Sikh religious body, the Shiromani Gurdwara Parbandhak Committee (SGPC).

I was seething with anger and was certain that this inquiry had been conducted to take revenge on me. And that it would continue with them finding new ways to harass me in the future.

I also resolved to pay them back in the same coin with interest. An opportunity was coming my way, as another secret report was about to be leaked that would expose the whole charade behind the clean chit given to Sharma by Malhotra. And that sensational report was the Bali Report.

17

Bali Report Unveiled

1 June 2003

Sunday

Ideally, a clean chit to Sharma shouldn't have affected me much. As a journalist, I need to be impartial. It is true that the news ought to have been telecast on a 'told as it happened' basis, yet my moral responsibility as a reporter was to evoke curiosity in public minds, to seek the truth beyond the perceived reality painted in the government's narratives.

After a few days, I recovered from the disappointment caused by the clean chit. During that period, I pondered over the possible government processes that may have worked in Sharma's favour and enabled him to get an easy and quick clean chit. I then activated my sources in the police department. I found out that as per the protocol, a report like Jaiswal's is forwarded by the DGP to the additional DGP (law and order) for his review. The DGP is the head of the state police.

At the same time, Mandar received the news that Additional DGP (Law and Order) Om Prakash Bali had also prepared a review report on Jaiswal's report and sent it to DGP Subash Malhotra for review, but DGP Malhotra had sidelined it. This news was confirmed but with the matter being all over the place, sourcing the new report was a tough task. This was headline-worthy news, but could not be telecast on TV without the report in hand. I had a good estimate of what kind of legal trouble I could land into at the slightest mistake, owing to my reporting history with the bruised police force. The whole month of May was spent mulling over the viability of getting my hands on the Bali Report. Contacting Bali or Malhotra for the same may have raised their antennas and with that, any possibility to get the report would have been nipped in the bud. On 30 May, I finally managed to obtain the report through my source.

Om Prakash Bali had made the following observations in his report:

1. A number of loose ends have been left in the investigation, which are glaring enough to indicate that they can only be suspicious and mala fide, to say the least. The burden of default has to be borne

by officers Deshmukh, Mulani, Jadhav and Mushrif for their various acts of omission and commission and intent. It appears that the evidence was not marshalled properly, certain accused were included and dropped at will without bringing up even an iota of evidence to justify the action of investigation officer on record.

2. The DGP office instructed then commissioner of Pune, R.S. Sharma, to evoke MCOCA in this case. Even though the investigative officer had sent his proposal on 9 July 2002, the final approval was granted only two months later, on 3 September 2002, thus causing tremendous damage to the investigation and probable outcome of the case.

3. As regards the role of Pune Police Commissioner R.S. Sharma, I am in full agreement with findings on the acts of omission and commission on his part as brought up by Subodh Jaiswal. Apart from this, it becomes very clear that R.S. Sharma was fully in the picture about the progress of investigation on day-to-day basis. He, however, appears to have failed to keep proper control over the investigation for reasons best known to him. The documents of the investigation disclose that everything possible was done to ensure, among other things, that sufficient evidence is not marshalled so as to benefit the accused. The investigation done by the team of officers under him has been, to say the least,

very shoddy. R.S. Sharma cannot plead ignorance about the defective investigation as the same was conducted in consultation with him on day-to-day basis and as such, he is equally responsible for the act of omission and commission of the officers named in the inquiry report. When an officer is prepared to take mileage out of so-called good detective work, he must also be prepared to face the flak for the failure to investigate the case properly.

4. Though the initial detection was very good, the investigation of the case was shoddy and full of shortcomings for which the responsibility has to be shared by R.S. Sharma along with his subordinates.

5. I must commend the excellent work done by Subodh Jaiswal and his team in not only carrying out thorough and painstaking investigation and chargesheeting within time limits, but also for carrying out inquiry into allegations made by Mushrif in a detailed and systematic manner without any let or hindrance.

The last page of the report had the signature of O.P. Bali and the date mentioned was 12 April 2003. It was evidently clear that R.S. Sharma had been given a clean chit despite the recommendations to take action, not only by Jaiswal but also by Sharma's superior, O.P. Bali, in their reports. Not only that, O.P. Bali's report was kept under wraps and no one had any clue about it.

I felt that this was an act of blatantly betraying the public. This report had been deliberately restricted. Media and public were blindfolded on the fate of the matter and it all happened in the name of maintaining secrecy. Now was the time to understand the significance and applicability of transparency or right to information.§ This was a blazing example of how high-ranked officials and politicians repressed certain pivotal information from coming to the public's ambit.

When DGP Malhotra was contacted, he did not deny the existence of this report. His response was, 'My service conduct rules do not conform to discussing the department's internal matters with the media.'

I asked him a question: 'Does this report exist?'

'I do not wish to give any comment on this matter,' Malhotra responded. Malhotra was unable to either deny or accept it. Disgruntled at the leak of the report, he was clearly stressed and fuming. His anger was valid, as this meant questions being raised him were based on proof.

Home Minister and Deputy Chief Minister Chhagan Bhujbal handed over the baton to DGP Malhotra. Bhujbal stated the following during a packed press conference: 'I have no information on if a Bali Report was written and in case it has indeed been written, then it hasn't reached me yet. You ask DGP Malhotra.' Further, Bhujbal said in

---

§ The Right to Information Act was not in existence at the time of the first edition of this book.

a caustic manner, 'If there is a report, you will get it first. I may be the home minister, but why would I get the report? It is your obligation to procure the report and show it.'

Next day was Sunday. On 1 June 2003, NDTV began to telecast this report from seven in the morning, whereas Mandar Parab, who had access to this report before me, had his channel show the report at 2 p.m. on the same day.

Around one in the afternoon, I got a call from a police inspector, Narendra Singh. Within police quarters, rumours were rife about Narendra Singh being part of R.S. Sharma's inner coterie. I knew him well. He called me on my mobile and said, 'Sanjay! What mischief are you up to? You showed another report against Sir. Why are you even doing this? You are our own man, brother. Despite being from our UP, you are still doing all this!'

I said, 'See, Narendra. First of all, I did not write the report. O.P. Bali wrote it. I am only showing it on TV. If I won't, some other channel will. Or tomorrow some paper will print it.'

But he had his own counterarguments. 'No! No one else will do it. Everyone says Sanjay Singh is leading all of it. If he stops, no one else will pursue it.'

'This is a misunderstanding. You can influence some journalists to be on your side but not all of them. Someone will report it someday,' I replied.

'Sanjay, you do one thing. Stop further telecast of the report and meet Sharma sir at once.' He had probably vowed to not comprehend reality.

I answered stoically, 'Report telecasts will not stop at any cost. It will be broadcast until tomorrow morning. As for the meeting with Sharma, I am ready to meet him and even conduct his interview.'

He understood I was a tough nut to crack. He disconnected the phone immediately and this was the last I heard from him. He never spoke to me again.

After a few weeks, he was arrested by the Anti-Corruption Bureau in a bribery case.

Two months later, the state government gave a clarification to the courts that DGP Malhotra had shared no information related to O.P. Bali's report with them and as it is the Bali Report was an internal matter of the police department.

18

Public Interest Litigation

8 June 2003

Saturday

In the meantime, Mandar and I continued to meet. After all the discussions and deliberations, we arrived at the conclusion that filing a PIL was the only way to enable this matter to move forward.

After collating all the relevant documents and information, we created a broad framework of action by conducting a thorough study of all the aspects related to the case.

We chanced upon Mushrif in Mumbai one day. We again suggested that he approach the court. But Mushrif was adamant on his old stance of lodging a criminal complaint at the Pune police station against R.S. Sharma.

We told Mushrif a police complaint would be of no use, as the legal procedures of the police system weren't robust enough to grab the neck of one of their own.

Mandar suggested to Mushrif that he should either file a petition himself, or have someone else file a PIL. In our opinion, approaching the court was the sole option that might help—a PIL at the Mumbai court felt like the only way forward in this matter.

In the last ten years or so, many cases have come to light in which courts played a prominent role in helping people attain justice. In hindsight, such incidents do kick off debates over the rights of the judiciary and blur the boundaries between the legal, executive and legislative powers.

Journalists often go silent after filing their report, assuming their role is over. In a conundrum, we thought, were we to follow the same precedent? Or should we play an active role in escalating this fraudulence to the courts? Weaving and unweaving our dilemma, we ended up studying the matter from a legal point of view too.

During news coverage, we often ran into the famous lawyer Majeed Memon. We consulted him on the legal aspects of this case. Memon had earned considerable name and fame as a criminal lawyer in the last ten years and was enthused by this case. He believed that the matter was being repressed. In his professional interest, Memon took some documents and information from us.

We kept thinking there must be someone who could become the petitioner. Everyone could not stay immune forever. We both were salaried people—we were not autonomous, thus could not become the petitioners. The other reason was that if we did become petitioners, then it would be unethical to report on the case thereafter. It would also be against the fundamentals of journalism.

We also met Nikhil Wagle during this process. The unequivocal editor of *Mahanagar* newspaper played a pivotal role in having the petition against Salman Khan in the car accident case filed. Wagle had a distinctive image as an audacious journalist. Despite facing the wrath of a political party like the Shiv Sena, he refused to bow down. His newspaper's circulation may have been limited, but he was counted amongst the forces to reckon with in modern journalism.

We showed Wagle some of the documents during our meeting. As a newspaper editor, Wagle knew about a few things already. We briefed him on the finer nuances of the case. By the end of our discussion, Wagle was in complete sync with our view that the judiciary was the last resort to expose the shenanigans unfolding in the case. He agreed initially, but later, owing to certain personal reasons, Wagle declined to be the petitioner.

Similarly, one day, we met Yogesh Pratap Singh. Y.P. Singh was a sharp-witted IPS officer with a clean image. His superiors and politicians were wary of his brutally straightforward nature. This was the reason his promotions were delayed and for years, he served tenures in low-value unimportant postings. But he enjoyed goodwill with people and journalists. We knew Y.P. Singh well. Before him, we had also requested former Police Commissioner Julio Ribeiro to be the petitioner, but were met with disappointment. Our resolve was failing. Suddenly, Majeed Memon gave us some good news, one day. The news was that Anna Hazare had contacted him to file a PIL.

Anna Hazare was a self-styled Gandhian leader. He was known for his simple lifestyle and clarity of thought. Specially popular for his anti-corruption mass movement against the Shiv Sena–BJP government or the one that came after, the Congress–NCP government. Hazare came down hard on prevalent corruption issues during tenures of both governments, causing the people of Maharashtra to view him as a social reformer and anti-corruption crusader.

Finally, Anna Hazare filed a PIL on 10 June.

Before this, Mukesh Vashi had filed a petition in January, in which he had requested for a CBI inquiry into the whole matter.

Hazare's petition sought some of the following prayers to issue appropriate writ, direction or order, under Article 226 of the Indian Constitution:

1. Asking state government to explain what action had been taken against the erring police officer.
2. Asking Maharashtra government, the home ministry, additional chief secretary and DGP to take deterrent punitive action against the guilty police officers as recommended in the Jaiswal Report, or alternatively, any other appropriate action which the court may deem fit.

3. Asking Maharashtra government, home ministry, additional chief secretary and DGP to initiate civil and criminal action against the police officers who had been indicted in inquiry report as under IPC.
4. Requesting for the production of telephone recordings of Telgi with the corrupt policemen, which had been recorded by Karnataka Police.
5. Action against police officials like R.S. Sharma and Mulani before their retirement, which was due in the near future.
6. Transfer of the guilty and indicted officials to non-executive postings.

Anna Hazare's PIL received much publicity and the fight gained momentum with his advent on to the battlefield.

Post Hazare's petition, all kinds of talks surfaced. People who were negatively influenced by the petition began spreading lies. Majeed Memon confirmed this as well. One evening, when we reached his home, he looked distressed. He was most perturbed at being labelled a lawyer from a specific community or a lawyer representing the underworld. The rumour mill was churning statements like 'Hazare is still all right, but having a lawyer like Majeed Memon can be detrimental to the case'.

That day, Memon asked us if we would prefer a bigger lawyer to represent the matter, in order to put such vitriolic rumour-mongering to rest. But in the end, we all agreed it was best to stick with him (Memon later became MP in the Rajya Sabha and the chief spokesperson of the NCP). Majeed Memon is a highly emotional man. This works for him sometimes and at other times, goes against him. His arguments have an emotional edge which is evident in the court. Majeed wanted to bring the Congress–NCP government to the witness stand, especially the NCP-controlled home ministry.

Mandar and I felt Hazare's petition had missed a few vital points that needed attention, such as:

1. Make DCP Ankush Shinde's investigation report public, which details charges of malfeasance against Mumbai crime branch.
2. The state should place on record what actions were taken against the erring officers.
3. The SIT should be made free from government control and the inquiry must be monitored by the court.

To draw attention to the aforementioned points, we felt the need to file another PIL.

Mandar and I were sitting at an Irani hotel near the sessions court when we chanced upon Ashwin Bhalekar and Prashant Surve. Both were lawyers by profession. Bhalekar and Mandar were school and college mates. A young legal professional duo, Ashwin and Prashant were like Jai and Veeru from the iconic Hindi movie *Sholay*. They dreamt of achieving something big in life. And on top of that, they were both mavericks like us. Sometimes, they fought cases au gratis. They hadn't been able to become one of those affluent lawyers, and if things continued in this manner, they never would.

Over rounds of tea, Bhalekar spotted the Telgi case-related papers and started a discussion on the matter. We shared our theory of adding the leftover points to another PIL. Bhalekar and Surve agreed with our point of view after reviewing the documents for themselves.

They also wanted to watch the truth unfold in this case. Prashant Surve showed interest in filing the PIL. Prashant shared how deeply invested he was in the case, and how he had all newspaper cuttings related to the case in a file folder. Ashwin was in agreement with him. But Prashant wanted to study the legal aspects of all the points we had made before making a decision. We suggested they file a PIL and took their leave.

After two days, out of the blue, Mandar called me. He said Ashwin Bhalekar and Prashant Surve had asked us to meet them along with the papers related to the Telgi case. We went to Bhalekar's house that night and handed over the required documents. Surve was also present there. Bhalekar said he would be the advocate on record for the case and Prashant Surve, the petitioner. They both made a resolve to own this case.

Ashwin prepared and showed us the draft for our opinion. We gave our inputs and Bhalekar weaved them together in legal language. Bhalekar said he would burn the midnight oil to prepare all the documents in order to file the petition in the Bombay High Court the very next day. This would enable timely dispatch of the petition's copies to all the accountable parties. We took their leave way past midnight and headed to our respective homes.

The next morning, Bhalekar filed the PIL. Copies were dispatched to all the accountable parties and the list of the thirteen involved included the chief minister of Maharashtra, Deputy Chief Minister Chhagan Bhujbal, SIT chief Subodh Jaiswal, then police commissioner of Mumbai R.S. Sharma, DIG S.M. Mushrif, joint commissioner of Pune Mahesh Gauri, SP Mulani and PI Prakash Deshmukh.

Bhalekar was the on-record advocate in Prashant Surve's petition but the role of senior council was played by Vijay Thorat. Senior advocate Vijay Thorat, the man who tackled the government for their lacklustre treatment of the Telgi case, was appointed Maharashtra's advocate general after a year.

Adhering to the administrative and legal procedures became instrumental in getting periodic dates in the high court. In the meantime, two more PILs were filed. All petitions were collated and a collective hearing was initiated for the matter. It was under the sharp scrutiny of the courts and set the wheels in motion. Court vigilance accelerated the government machinery and investigators' pace of work. The court's directives had a positive impact on the investigations. Some of the orders passed were as follows:

Order of 23 July 2003

M.C. Mulani, assistant commissioner of police, was due to retire from service on 31 August 2003. The government acceded to the fact that though there were recommendations to place Mulani under suspension, pending disciplinary proceedings, no action was taken. Mulani was eventually suspended before retirement due to the court's intervention.

The government was directed to file an affidavit for dealing with all the dubious conduct officials, who were involved in the cases registered against Telgi between 1995 and 1998.

Order of 4 September 2003

The order of the court dated 4 September 2003 recorded the following:

- The State of Maharashtra should strengthen the Special Investigation Team (SIT) by appointing more officers so that investigation may be expedited.
- It is agreed by all the parties that such investigation may be conducted under the supervision of Mr S.S. Puri, retired Director General of Police.
- SIT will make investigations and report about the culpability of officer(s) howsoever his/their rank may be.

- SIT will also make investigations and report about culpability of officers of private companies as well as public sector undertakings.
- SIT to take appropriate steps/actions for getting transcript of the tape-recorded conversation produced in the criminal court in the state of Karnataka.

Order of 15 October 2003

Since the Mumbai police commissioner R.S. Sharma was retiring on 30 November, keeping this in mind, the Bombay High Court instructed SIT chief S.S. Puri to expedite the investigations on Sharma's role in the case. The court order clearly stated, 'Mr S.S. Puri should consider about the involvement of R.S. Sharma, keeping in mind that Mr Sharma is due to retire on November 30, 2003.'

The court also instructed Karnataka SIT chief to hand over the transcript of the tape-recorded conversation with Telgi within two weeks, to the Mumbai SIT chief.

Order of 3 November 2003

Karnataka Police was dragging its feet in handing over the telephonic conversation transcript. They were apprehensive about the conversations on tapes possibly being leaked, which might jeopardize the entire investigation. The lawyer representing Karnataka also said that the talks were elaborate, and it might take up to a year to transcribe them. But the court refuted the Karnataka government's plea and instructed them to, 'Hand over the transcript and the conversation tapes on as is basis to the Maharashtra SIT.'

Court Order of 12 November 2003

The report prepared by S.S. Puri on R.S. Sharma was presented in the court, but Advocate General Goolam Vahanvati suggested that the confidential report may be sent to the chief minister of Maharashtra, and only he may decide the course of action on the same. The Bombay High Court acceded to the advocate general's suggestion.

In his report, S.S. Puri found R.S. Sharma guilty on nine accounts.

Under the directive and close vigilance of the court, the SIT was free from any coercion from either the government or senior police officials. They had the autonomy to conduct impartial investigations without any influences. The ball was now in the SIT's court and they were preparing for a litmus test of their work.

I thought of finding sources within the SIT. The first name that came to my mind was DIG Subodh Jaiswal's.

19

A Meeting with DIG Jaiswal

11 June 2003

Wednesday

It might come as a surprise to many that I was yet to meet DIG Jaiswal. The same officer who had penned such a sensational report, recommended action against his senior officers, and exposed the nexus between corrupt police officials and Telgi.

I called Subodh Jaiswal's home. When he came on the phone, I said, 'This is Sanjay Singh from NDTV. I wanted to meet you.'

'Please come to the office', was the response from the other end.

I thought he may have missed hearing my name in our conversation. I pressed on, 'This is Sanjay Singh ... NDTV journalist. Would it be appropriate to meet publicly at your office?'

The voice responded, 'Oh! Is that you? I have no desire to meet you. There is enough stress in my life. I do not want to add more to it because of you.' Jaiswal comprehended my complete introduction only now. 'I cannot meet you.' Saying this, he disconnected the phone.

I tried my best to placate him, but he disconnected the phone.

I thought, what a stubborn man he was! But I am also a man of resolve. I had a deep desire to meet him, extract information and quench my curiosity. After two days, I landed up at Subodh Jaiswal's office. Jaiswal's office was located in the ground floor of the Mumbai Police headquarters. I handed over my business card to Jaiswal's peon. Taking the card, the peon said he would pass it on to Jaiswal, but that he didn't entertain any journalists. He had refused to meet many in the past. This statement further dimmed the prospect of my meeting Jaiswal. As it is, after our dismal telephonic interaction, I was most doubtful Jaiswal would allow me any audience whatsoever. But journalism teaches one a lesson in humility after contempt. Many times, we approach politicians or policemen without prior appointments. There are many moments of awkwardness or embarrassment endured by journalists. That pain is not visible on the screen or in newspapers to either the editor or the public consuming the news. They are least bothered about the process. It is only the news that matters.

I waited outside Jaiswal's office for half an hour. Finally, he called me in. My wish was granted. I finally was face to face with the man to whom I owed my biggest news story. But I was mistaken about not having met him before. In the year 1999, I had met Jaiswal in Goa while working for Zee News. He was then posted in the prime minister's security agency, Special Protection Group (SPG), and we had had a brief interaction during my visit to interview the prime minister.

I reminded Subodh Jaiswal (who in the coming years would be appointed Mumbai police commissioner, DGP of Maharashtra, DG Central Industrial Security Force (CISF) and also spend a few years at Research and Analysis Wing (RAW) and in 2021, be appointed chief of CBI) of our last meeting. Jaiswal paused and spoke of a faint recall, though his face said otherwise. He greeted me awkwardly. I could sense hostility in his demeanour and felt like an unwelcome guest.

He clarified at the beginning of our conversation. 'I will not discuss any matter related to the Telgi scam with you. Please have tea or coffee. We can indulge in some polite chit-chat.'

Damn! I cursed under my breath. That unreserved declaration killed the bleak hope of getting any kind of news out of the man. *How obstinate and ill-mannered!* I thought to myself.

During our conversation, Jaiswal apologized for his rude response on the phone. 'See, I was quite disturbed when you called earlier and could not talk properly. Post your telecast of my report, all fingers pointed at me out of suspicion that I had leaked the report. Everyone was suspicious of me and I had to bear the brunt of it, despite having no connection whatsoever with it.'

He was right. I had telecast the report without considering the repercussions for Jaiswal.

He continued, 'It shook me initially but I regained my composure later, when it was confirmed that none of my staff members or anyone from my office had leaked the report …'

I clarified from my end. 'Please know that it was imperative that the report came out. If we hadn't published the leaked report, the matter may have been repressed forever. Your senior officials and politicians may have buried it underground, and justice may have been denied to the wronged. In a way, whatever happened, happened for the best.'

'Whether the report would have been buried under the ground or not, I do not wish to debate over it. But I have no grievance against you now. What you did was right in its own way. You were just doing your job.' Jaiswal was treading cautiously with his measured sentences, so as not to get caught on the wrong foot.

His behaviour was justified. The environment created by his report on the Telgi scam investigation demanded disciplined behaviour and restricted reactions from him.

Dragging his own department to the courts and pointing fingers at his own superior officials warranted caution from his end. An air of toxicity hung over the police department in those days, eliciting mistrust amongst colleagues. The department was now divided into many factions and one specific group was working relentlessly to bring shame upon Jaiswal and his team. If I was in Jaiswal's place, I wouldn't have trusted anyone either, and yet he had agreed to talk to me.

Post our meeting, I adjudged Jaiswal as a hard-nosed, obstinate and belligerent person. What else can one say about a senior police official who maintained such an obnoxious outlook towards the media, despite being in the police force for seventeen or eighteen years? I was musing over this as I took Jaiswal's permission to leave. Somehow, I had a premonition that his hostility would eventually ease off. But it didn't. I met him again a few times, mostly during court hearings. During a random meeting, he shared how his workload had substantially increased due to the PIL filed in the Bombay High Court. Preparing reports for the court consumed considerable time. If the PIL were not there, the investigation work would have been faster.

Though I differed from his point of view. If it wasn't for the high court's active role, Jaiswal certainly wouldn't have been conducting his investigation in an impartial and stress-free environment. His senior officials and politicians would have caused upheaval in every possible manner to bury the matter. But Jaiswal was ostensibly struck by how the process might have been delayed with the arrest of larger fish in the pond, but it was nevertheless a start. The first arrest amongst policemen was that of Inspector Dilip Kamath, after which the process caught on.

20

And the Arrests Begin

Arrest of Politicians

The arrest of policemen had already become the talk of the town, but the imprisonment of two MLAs shifted focus to the political nexus of Telgi. With the Pandora's box now open, anything was possible. The matter had strong references of political alliances and the arrest of two MLAs was just the tip of the iceberg …

Anil Gote, MLA, Maharashtra

On 29 June 2003, Anil Gote, the MLA of Dhule, became the first politician to be arrested in the Telgi case.

Anil Gote was a known face in Maharashtra's manipulative politics. This lone MLA from the Samajwadi Janata Party was close to all political parties. Amongst others, he was a close aide of former Prime Minister Chandra Shekhar, and the renowned lawyer Ram Jethmalani.

As per the chargesheet, Gote was closely associated with Telgi and used his political connections to favour him in exchange for pecuniary benefits and undue economic advantages from the illegal activities of Telgi's crime syndicate. The information in the chargesheet throws more light on the matter:

1. The Kisan Trust was founded by Anil Gote. One of the main conditions to become a member of the trust was that one had to be a Dhule resident to become a trustee. In order to overcome this hurdle, Telgi had given Anil Gote's Dhule home address as his local address.

2. When an account of the Kisan Trust was scrutinized, it was revealed that the accounts had been fabricated and the funds supplied by Telgi had deliberately been camouflaged using false receipts in the name of prominent personalities like Ram Jethmalani and Lalit Suri (both MPs) and when both Jethmalani and Suri were questioned, they flatly denied having made any donations to the Kisan Trust. So the logical conclusion was Telgi had donated twenty-six lakh rupees to the trust headed by Gote, out of which he created fraudulent receipts of five lakh each in the names of former minister

Ram Jethmalani and Lalit Suri, and the remaining 16 lakh in the names of eight others without their knowledge.

3. Almost two years after a Mumbai court declared Telgi an escaped convict, on 16 January 1996, Telgi and Anil Gote were spotted together on the same stage at a Kisan Trust public programme in Dhule.

4. Investigation revealed that in 1994, it was Anil Gote who had used his political clout to obtain the stamp vendor licence for Telgi. Gote also requested the electricity board to give rebate to Telgi on his pending electricity bills worth 3.64 lakh rupees and allow him to pay them in ten instalments.

5. During scrutiny of documents seized in June 2002 in a raid at Telgi's office (Botawala Chambers, Fort, Mumbai), fake stamps and stamp papers worth 140 crore were seized, along with one copy of a letter on the letterhead of Ram Jethmalani (Union minister for urban affairs and employment) dated 2 June 1998 addressed to Yashwant Sinha (Union finance minister). When Ram Jethmalani was asked about this letter, he stated that Anil Gote had brough Telgi to him for recommending Ganga Prakash (then deputy GM, Indian Security Press, Nashik) for a promotion and on Gote's request, Jethmalani had forwarded the said letter to Yashwant Sinha for his consideration.

The SIT concluded that during 1997 to 2003, Telgi paid all hotel bills for Anil Gote's stay at Hotel Ritz, Mumbai. Telgi also paid twice for Gote's Delhi trips.

Gote's arrest shook the Maharashtra political circles to the core. Until yesterday, Gote was everyone's best friend. Today, everyone was maintaining distance from him, calling their alliance with him a political formality. The ruling Congress–NCP alliance referred to BJP leader Gopinath Munde as sharing close proximity with Gote. They accused Gote of conspiring for a political coup along with BJP–Shiv Sena, in an attempt to bring down the state government in June 2002. The opposition was in shock and went on the back foot. The BJP's senior leader Gopinath Munde became answerable to the questions raised by the journalists.

Along with the opposition, there were allegations against the ruling Congress Party, as in the year 1994, when Telgi was issued the stamp vending licence, it was ruling the state. The allegations from both sides were authentic, but their long-term repercussions were yet to be felt.

In court, Gote refuted the SIT's allegations and claimed innocence. Gote may have been Telgi's friend, but the other MLA, Krishna Yadav, had been out on the hunt for Telgi, and fell prey himself in the process.

Krishna Yadav, MLA, Andhra Pradesh

Abdul Karim Telgi had one home in South Bombay in Karim Court Building, Colaba. The SIT raided this house on 19 January 2003 and an audiotape was recovered which left them in a quandary. The cassette had a recorded conversation between Telgi and a politician, Krishna Yadav. Krishna Yadav was an Andhra Pradesh MLA from Hyderabad's Himayatnagar area. The strongman MLA from the Telugu Desam Party had also formerly served as a labour minister. The contents of the tape had shocked the SIT. As per the chargesheet, during the taped conversation, Krishna Yadav had demanded two crore rupees from Telgi, but the deal had to be settled at five lakh rupees.

After this, the SIT started investigating Krishna Yadav. They discovered how old Yadav and Telgi's alliance was. In 1998, Krishan Yadav had abducted two members of Telgi's gang, Abdul Wahid and Sadashiv, which had caused a hindrance in Telgi's scam operation in Andhra Pradesh. The negotiations for setting both of them free were held at the premises of the Andhra Pradesh assembly. Both were released from the same premises, post the recovery of a sum from Telgi.

But Telgi had planted a noose around his perpetrator. He had recorded his conversation with Yadav. In the end, the small-minded politician's sharp wit failed in front of Telgi's, the king of all scams.

The SIT arrested Yadav on 6 September 2003. Yadav denied all the charges levelled against him. After many years, he was granted bail.

Arrest of Policemen

Dilip Kamath, Assistant Inspector, Mumbai Crime Branch

On 12 June 2003, Mandar and I were discussing the Telgi case in the press room, when we met Sub Inspector Sachin Vaze—the same person who had made the cautionary call to me about my 16 April news report on Pradeep Sawant. Vaze had a unique ability of adding weight and volume to his statements, irrespective of their authenticity or validity. Kamath was arrested the next day, i.e., 13 June 2003. I shared the news with Vaze.

This was the first police arrest in the Telgi matter, and his role as disclosed in the chargesheet made one wonder how his contrived mind could have given seasoned criminal minds a run for their money. Some of his devious acts were as follows:

1. Kamath and Telgi's nexus started in December 1998, when Kamath caught a racket of Telgi's. Kamath wilfully and intentionally did not carry out the investigation and diverted its track of investigation towards a non-existent person named Murugan. Kamath, who was the investigation officer of that particular case, made this deliberate omission with the intention of protecting Telgi. Despite knowing

that Telgi was a proclaimed and wanted offender in three different police stations in Mumbai, Kamath did not take legal action against him.

2. Telgi was arrested in November 2001 by Karnataka Police. Kamath found out that Telgi was being held at a Bangalore jail and decided to take advantage of this. He established contact with Telgi with the help of his lawyer. With the intention to extract crores of rupees from the racket, he went to meet Telgi illegally and without authority, at the jail in July 2002 and had a secret discussion. Both of them conceived a plan together. At Telgi's behest, a raid was conducted at Rais Khan's house in Hyderabad by Kamath. Rais Khan was not there at the time, but the police recovered ten bags of fake stamps. Upon his return to Mumbai, Kamath declared that six bags containing stamps worth 3.67 crore rupees had been found during the raid. The other four bags taken charge of by Kamath remained untraced and were believed to have been destroyed or sold in the market. After three months, Rais Khan was caught by Kamath, who did not show his arrest and unauthorizedly brought him to Mumbai by air from Hydrabad, booking his flight ticket under a fictitious name, Salim S. Later, Rais Khan was let go after taking a bribe of seven lakh rupees.

3. In July 2002, Kamath arrested Telgi's accomplice, Syed Hameed. Kamath took Hameed unauthorizedly to Hyderabad. They stayed at Hotel Golkonda, where Kamath took an eight lakh rupee bribe from Hameed's wife with a promise to abstain from taking further lawful measures in the said investigation.

4. On 27 October 2002, Kamath took over custody of Telgi from Bangalore Police in a murder case, acting as a representative of the Mumbai crime branch. Instead of taking Telgi to the lockup, he took him to Hotel Rajhans in Chembur, where four rooms were booked for them. Then he struck up a partnership with Telgi. Technically, Telgi may have been in custody, but he did not spend even a single day in the lockup. For eighty-five days, he stayed at his 7 Cuffe Parade home, or Sunny House, in Colaba, or at Hotel Ashray in Sion, from where Telgi was not only still operating his illegal racket but was also meeting real estate agents to dispose of some of his properties in Mumbai. Telgi had purchased a chemical plant under the name of Thane Polyorganics Ltd at Turbhe and while he was being held in his custody, Kamath took him to the said chemical plant for aiding and abetting him in disposing of the said property.

5. In one of the cases (Cuffe Parade police station CR No. 382/95), Officer Kamath, despite being present in the courtroom, did not inform the magistrate that Telgi was a proclaimed offender in the same case since 1996, nor did he produce the collected evidence in court to oppose Telgi's bail. Thus, he facilitated Telgi to obtain bail in one of the cases.

6. But on 9 January 2003, the secret of Telgi's lavish lifestyle was unearthed, when the joint SIT of Maharashtra and Karnataka found him whiling away his time at home. Post this, Maharashtra SIT chief DIG Jaiswal presented a report related to the raid to the government. To save their skin, Kamath and the crime branch chose to piggyback on Telgi. On Telgi's directive, they recovered fake stamps worth 830 crore rupees from a godown near Bhiwandi, and earned accolades in the media. This was done with the intention of protecting Dilip Kamath and his associate policemen from departmental action following the 10 January report by Jaiswal—just to escape backlash. Kamath also omitted Telgi's association with this raid at the Bhiwandi godown. And this turned out to be the Achilles' heel in this case, leading to many arrests later. To save Telgi, Kamath attributed the abovementioned seizure to one Shabbir Ahmad

Shaikh, by creating an imaginary story in official records, purportedly recording a statement by Shabbir and Ram Ratan Soni (Telgi's guru from his initial days). Shabbir, once Telgi's small-time operative, was also targeted because he had given a confessional statement under MCOCA implicating Telgi in two cases, one of which was the Christopher Bhatti murder case.

7. Kamath alone received a total of 96.5 lakh rupees as bribe (illegal gratification) from Telgi and his syndicate by abusing his position.

8. On Telgi's directive, he recovered 33 lakh rupees from four different witnesses, which were proceeds from Telgi's crime, but showed recovery of only 1.5 lakh rupees, pocketing the balance amount of 31.5 lakh.

9. Kamath visited Karnataka and Goa illegally with the under-arrest Telgi, who bore all the travel cost and luxury hotel expenses. In November 2002, Kamath, along with a few other policemen unauthorizedly took Telgi to his native place Khanapur (in Karnataka) by road and stayed in Hotel Sanman, Belgaum. Then they further travelled to Goa, and Telgi and the policemen stayed at Dona Sylvia Hotel, giving fictitious names in hotel records. Dilip Kamath along with his family members were lodged

at a seven-star hotel, The Leela Palace, where a two days' bill back in 2002 came to ₹52,600. All the expenses of Karnataka and Goa trips were borne by Telgi. The Goa–Mumbai airfare for all policemen and Telgi himself was also paid by the latter.

10. During the five months July–November 2002, the amount spent on all unauthorized air travel by Officer Kamath and others, worked out to be around 1.9 lakh rupees and this was all paid by Telgi.

For the crime branch, Kamath's arrest was the first sign or rather, the first omen of the danger that lay ahead. The same MCOCA that had been a sharp weapon to slay underworld syndicates was used to arrest a crime branch official this time. But this action also indicated the future behind bars which awaited other accused police officials in the matter, for Kamath's arrest was only the first amongst many others to follow.

The day after Kamath's arrest, former Joint Commissioner Sridhar Wagal, during whose tenure Mumbai Police crime branch had milked Telgi unabashedly, visited the crime branch. He held a two-hour-long, highly secretive meeting behind closed doors, with Joint Commissioner Satyapal Singh. What transpired between Singh and Wagal that day was never disclosed.

Datta Dhal, Police Inspector, Mumbai Crime Branch

Kamath's arrest had given sleepless nights to Mumbai Police crime branch. Everyone was aware that the arrests of the accused policemen were now imminent. After Kamath, next in the natural sequence of arrest was Datta Dhal.

As per the chargesheet, Datta Dhal was in-charge of Mumbai Police's Dharavi unit and Dilip Kamath reported to him. He granted him the autonomy to extract as much as he desired from Telgi. He was an equal partner in all the crimes committed by Kamath. There were seven cases registered against Telgi in Mumbai, and all were transferred to Crime Branch Unit 5 Joint Commissioner (Crime) Sridhar Wagal. Datta Dhal was in-charge of this unit and did not allow the respective investigation officers (IOs) to investigate in detail, abusing his official position to not carry out investigation properly and logically.

As per the chargesheet, Dhal allowed Dilip Kamath to unauthorizedly visit Bangalore to meet Telgi. Dhal was accused of aiding and abetting both Telgi and Kamath. It was his unit which gained custody of Telgi and while in custody, Telgi stayed at his own home or at a hotel, and ran his business smoothly using a mobile phone and meeting with his associates. Datta Dhal was arrested on 21 August

2003. He was granted bail after spending eleven months in jail. Later, he was instated.

Vasisth Andhale

Andhale's arrest was certain. Almost everyone, including Andhale, was aware of this fact.

As per the chargesheet, on 20 May 2002, Inspector Vasisth Andhale was posted at Mumbai Police Crime Branch's airport unit, and along with his team, conducted raids on two hideouts of Telgi's around Mumbai Fort and the Andheri area, recovering fake stamps worth fifty lakh rupees. He arrested and brought twelve people to his unit office, but released all of them after taking bribes. Andhale was arrested on 18 October 2003 and was granted bail after nine months.

ACP Gokul Patil and Kakade

In the year 1999, during an investigation, Assistant Police Commissioner Gokul Patil and Sub Inspector Kakade of Mira Road police station, Thane, had found Telgi's hideouts at Fort and Mulund, where he used to print fake stamps. They neither conducted a raid at these locations, nor made any attempts to recover any of the counterfeit documents. They willingly sheltered Telgi's wrongdoings and showed no inclination to arrest him.

The SIT arrested both of them on 18 October 2003.

SP Mulani

Mulani was also arrested in December 2003. His misdeeds have been explained in detail in Jaiswal Report, quoted earlier in the book.

21
Remorse of the Encounter Specialist

Since the report was exposed, our phones were being tapped, or at least the possibility of this constantly plagued our minds. The arrest of policemen and politicians had created an unspoken fear amongst the police force, but our hearts trembled with fear of other possibilities.

Whenever any policeman called us, he kept communication brief. And the ones who would agree to speak with us at length, insisted upon switching phones before opening up. Different voices emanated from our phones. All the signs and indications of phone tapping as detailed by our policemen colleagues were there. We weren't surprised at the discovery. The journalists covering the crime beat were aware of the illegal phone tapping of many journalists by a specific unit of the Mumbai Police

Crime Branch. This clearly established the existence of a parallel crime branch being run by a specific faction.

We also began to exercise caution and started using the landline for our conversations. We brought prepaid SIM cards and started changing numbers frequently.

As if this wasn't enough, I once got a call from Star News reporter, Jitendra Dixit. He said he wanted to meet me immediately. I met him at his home in the afternoon. He looked petrified. He said a journalist named Prabhat had met him and threatened him, saying, 'Whatever you people are doing against the police is not right. You have no idea about the power the police holds. Police can sometimes plant weapons at people's homes and if those weapons are recovered from homes, then MCOCA can be evoked. It is a tough law and grants monstrous power to the police.'

Prabhat's statement had troubled Dixit greatly. Dixit suspected it was not a mere statement but a direct threat. Dixit said Prabhat was a close aide of Crime Branch's high-profile leader DCP Pradeep Sawant. Almost all journalists were aware of this fact.

I was livid, but felt helpless in front of the illegal power centre at the Crime Branch. First and foremost, we removed sensitive documents from our homes so that they couldn't land us in trouble, should the police choose to raid our houses. We instructed people at home to never accept any gifts sent to our homes, at any time. The reason was clear. Mumbai Police was the self-proclaimed number two to Scotland Yard.

After two days, we came across Daya Nayak. (Encounter Specialist Daya Nayak, who was later arrested by the

Anti-Corruption Bureau (ACB) in the year 2006 in a disproportionate assets case and subsequently suspended. The Supreme Court quashed all charges levelled against him in the year 2010 and he was reinstated in the police force.)

Even though he was a mere sub inspector, his commanding air was of one no less than a commissioner. Five movies based on him were under production. He was deeply conscious of his image in the media and avoided direct confrontation with journalists. During our conversation, we started bad-mouthing Pradeep Sawant in front of him. We expressed our umbrage over the hint of threats sent our way. We lied about a report in the making that would shake the ground under DCP Sawant's feet. He tried to cajole us emotionally citing our friendship to know the details, but we refused to relent. We said we suspected he would pass the information on to DCP Sawant. The sole purpose behind lying was to take the bull by the horns and have him suffer the mental anguish we were enduring.

We met Daya Nayak twice, subsequently. He inquired about the report. We called it a classified document and shared nothing. As it is, what could one really share about a non-existent report?

But our lying worked. We got a chance to meet Pradeep Sawant within a week. We had gone to interview him regarding a news story. Mandar and a Zee News reporter, Calvin Joshua, were also there. After work drew to a close, Sawant addressed us, 'Listen, Daya Nayak mentioned you all were upset over something.'

Our trick was working. Unknowingly, Daya Nayak had served our purpose.

Sawant hesitated and proceeded with caution. 'See, there has been a misunderstanding. Please do not hold hard feelings in your heart. We misinterpreted the situation. I know we cannot be friends 365 days a year. It may also happen that our interests clash. Such is the nature of your job. If you report against us three to four days in a year, we also need to handle it wisely.'

Mandar, Calvin and I looked at each other.

'Sawant sir, the matter is not that simple. Everyone in the police department knows of your proximity to Prabhat. Whatever he says is considered to be as good as your word,' I said.

Mandar further said, 'First, he offered to arrange a weapon licence, then threatened incrimination and imprisonment under MCOCA. What does all of this mean, really?'

I continued, 'Prabhat is spreading rumours that I am going about selling copies of the Jaiswal Report for ₹10,000 apiece. Can he not comprehend this much that if money was the motive behind the report, then Sharma sir was the best client to extract lakhs of rupees from? Why go from door to door selling it?'

Sawant had no answer. The powerhouse of the Crime Branch we used to line up to interview was quietly bearing the brunt of the angst of three small-time journalists.

Mandar said, 'We have known you for years. Did things ever escalate to this level? You need to understand that Jaiswal wrote the Jaiswal Report, Om Prakash Bali wrote the Bali Report, we did not write it. The SIT is conducting the investigation, not us! These are all policemen. As journalists, we are only mirroring what has been told already.'

I intervened and said, 'You are trying to shoot the messenger and not curb the message. If we do not cover this news, some other journalist will. The only difference is that we are reporting ahead of others. You can manage some reports for some time but you cannot control all the reports all the time. If this was the trend in this country, then ministers', even prime ministers' names wouldn't get dragged into scam controversies.'

Pradeep Sawant gave a patient hearing to our anger outburst. Then he said, 'Let bygones be bygones now. Let's bury the hatchet and make peace. We will take care not to repeat mistakes. If anything happens again, we will communicate directly to avoid any kind of misunderstanding.'

We did not say a word.

'All right. Please don't hold any hard feelings towards me,' he concluded. We left the place after getting our closure.

I do not think Sawant was satisfied by this interaction. Anyway, many a week passed without any policeman's arrest thereafter. The SIT was quiet, but it was only the calm before the storm, as the rank at which the next person to be arrested held, had never faced an arrest before. Not only Sawant—the upcoming arrest was enough to rob R.S. Sharma of his peace of mind.

22

IB to SIT

First Week of November 2003

A Mumbai Police constable and officer stationed at the checkpoint looked at me as if to say that a journalist was entering the building for the first time. A new IB building had been constructed at the Bandra Kurla Complex in Mumbai. Usually, IB people are like the ghosts who exist among us but remain invisible. Journalists have limited interaction with the IB and bare minimum contact with senior officials. On one of the upper floors, I was sitting across Sudhir Kumar (he went on to be appointed secretary (security) in the Cabinet Secretariat and thereafter, India's Vigilance Commissioner, whose jurisdiction covered Central government agencies, Central ministries, Central public sector undertakings (CPSUs), public sector banks and Centre-funded public institutes, etc.) after some time. He was the special director of IB's west zone and one of the four topmost intelligence officers in the country. In reality, this IPS officer was from the Maharashtra cadre, but he had been at the IB for the last two decades and had many accomplishments to his credit. It is said that there is no close comparison to his hold on matters related to Pakistan, counterterrorism operations and intelligent analysis. He also served on a diplomatic assignment in Germany.

A man with such a superlative biodata came across to me as simple, good-natured and courteous like any common man. It was difficult to fathom the respect his name evoked in the Maharashtra police force.

In the beginning of our conversation, he mentioned how Maharashtra Police carried out big encounters but never shared any credit with IB, where the complete behind-the-scenes work was conducted; local police was only like topping on the pizza. The encounter mentioned in the beginning of this book also came up during our discussion.

Kumar was an ace IB officer and it was evident that he knew of my relevance to the exposure of the Telgi scam. I shared with him that I did not have any source inside the investigating SIT, which restricted extraction of any related news. SIT chief S.S. Puri left no room for any information to filter out. He was being vigilant due to the sensitive nature of the probe and the involvement of police and politicians in the case. Another problem was not having a way for transferring any news I may have, past the SIT's closed doors. I estimated S.S. Puri to be acquainted with Sudhir Kumar, who was a senior of his from the Maharashtra cadre, and how that might pave the way for me.

Kumar heard me out patiently and suggested I try once again.

I had barely opened my mouth to voice my previous failed attempts, when he smiled and reiterated what he had said earlier. I must try once again.

I purposely chose late evening to visit the SIT office, a less news-relevant hour when the usual crowd of journalists would probably not be there. Usually, journalists hung around the road outside the SIT's Worli office, as there were strict restrictions in place to not allow anyone inside the gates. There was a message in my name at the gate to allow me in. As I entered, I met a visibly astonished cameraman Sunil Pudhari from another channel, waiting in the lobby. He was watching a journalist enter the SIT office for the first time. On the upper floor, as I was approaching S.S. Puri's office, I crossed paths with two people for a fraction of a second. The first was Subodh Jaiswal, whom I had met at his Maharashtra DGP office before. The other was DIG Hemant Nagrale (a few years later, Hemant Nagrale was appointed Mumbai police commissioner and Maharashtra DGP). Both senior officials had surprised expressions on their faces upon spotting a journalist (and that too, me) inside the SIT office.

I was delighted at the SIT chief agreeing to see me. As a journalist, my interest lay in knowing when the big fish in the pond, like prominent politicians and senior officers, would be caught. Till now, the SIT had only arrested MLAs and SPs. I was a bit greedy, so gathering more information on Telgi was also on my list. My meeting with S.S. Puri was cordial. Since it was our first meeting, there was mutual hesitancy and mild distrust, which eased into getting on friendly terms in subsequent meetings. I met S.S. Puri a few times again, once at the SIT office and twice at his home. It was not difficult to fathom what our conversations were all about.

23

Arrest of Sridhar Wagal

7 November 2003

Friday

Sridhar Wagal was joint commissioner of Mumbai from March 2002 to March 2003, and head of the Crime Branch. I had received news of Wagal being a suspected accused in this case. I was also aware of his efforts to save his skin by approaching a few politicians and officers at the state and Centre levels for help.

I had had the opportunity to meet Wagal a few days back, when state DGP Om Prakash Bali was retiring and the new DGP S.M. Shangari was taking charge. The programme was delayed and we had time in hand. Wagal's office was in the same DGP office complex. He was posted there as the

Arrest of Sridhar Wagal

head of the intelligence department. I had time to spare, so Mandar and I went to meet Wagal. Two more journalists joined us in Wagal's office. During our conversation, he left no stone unturned to criticize NDTV. He was upset at NDTV's vociferous telecast of the possibilities related to his arrest.

After a few days, on 7 November 2003, Wagal was arrested. This was the biggest arrest made so far. For the first time ever, an IPS officer was arrested under MCOCA.

It was the darkest day in its history for the police department. So far, only junior-level officers had been arrested in such cases; this was the first instance of a high-ranked police officer's arrest.

The chargesheet had the following allegations listed against Wagal:

1. On 8 June 2002, Pune Police instructed Wagal to investigate probable hiding places for the fake stamps, but to protect Telgi's interest, Wagal did not get the investigation done. Later, Pune Police seized fake stamps worth lakhs of rupees from the same hideouts and also confiscated stamp-printing machines.

2. Wagal and Pradeep Sawant had full knowledge of Inspector Kamath and Dhal's plan to extract money from Telgi. The recordings of telephonic conversations between Telgi, his lawyer Kulkarni and Inspector Kamath, substantiate this fact.

3. The Christopher murder case was solved and all the accused were arrested. Despite knowing this, the case was reopened only to gain custody of Telgi. During this time, the Kamath–Telgi nexus had started its operation and was in full knowledge of Wagal and DCP Sawant. (The details were shared along with allegations levelled against Kamath earlier.)

4. Mumbai Police had acquired Telgi's custody on the pretext of investigating the aforementioned murder case and the duo of Inspector Datta Dhal and Dilip Kamath were in-charge. Wagal transferred seven old cases related to Telgi to Dhal in haste, so that they (Kamat–Dhal) could retain Telgi in custody and milk him further. Wagal did not seek permission or inform the then police commissioner M.N. Singh before transferring the cases, which was completely against the rules. One of the intents behind transferring these cases was to weaken them and benefit Telgi. In lieu of Telgi enjoying a lavish lifestyle in custody, the process of earning the benefits in return, continued.(You have read about this before where the allegations against Inspector Kamath were detailed.)

5. One police inspector, I.M. Zahid, conducted a thorough investigation into a matter related to Telgi, during which he obtained details on Telgi's hideouts and his bank details. But Wagal showed

his displeasure at the investigation, which clearly shows that Wagal was trying to bury the evidence recovered.

6. Besides this, readers have already read about the 9 January 2003 raid and Telgi being found at his own home, followed by the recovery of fake stamp papers worth 830 crore rupees from Bhiwandi to cover up and escape embarrassment.

The day after his arrest, when Wagal was brought before the special MCOCA court, post his lawyer's argument, he stood up to plead his innocence, refuting all charges levelled against him.

Wagal's arrest sent shock down the spines of officials who had served under him. The erstwhile tigers on the prowl, the Crime Branch officers, were now trembling like wet cats. Whoever had a direct or indirect connection with Telgi's cases was suffering sleepless nights. Some were unable to bear this trauma and since our reporting was considered the bane causing this mayhem, the coming days were filled with terror for us as well. He was granted bail by the Supreme Court in 2007.

24

The Threat of November

24 November 2003

Monday

I reached home around 11.30 p.m. on 24 November and was preparing to sleep after my dinner, when my mobile rang. An unknown number flashed on my mobile screen: 022-25409950. Generally, a call this late meant an important news coming my way. I picked up.

'Hello?'

'Hello. Sanjay Singh speaking?' the voice from the other side asked.

'Yes, this is Sanjay Singh,' I responded.

The person on the other side, speaking in a Marathi accent started hurling the choicest abuses in Hindi and said, 'Your mother ... a ... motherfucker ... there is an itch in your ass, no? You are very fond of telecasting news, no? What you have done now ... you will repent for it for life. You, Dixit and Mandar Parab, you see what we do to force you all out of Mumbai. Your jobs are at stake. You just see what we do.' He spewed three or four more obscenities before disconnecting the line.

The man had been livid and aggressive. It disturbed me immensely. I looked at the number again. The number did not seem to be from my neighbourhood, but from Mulund or Thane. I thought it could have come from anywhere, but it was wise to check outside my house for any signs of danger. I was flabbergasted. Everyone at home was in a slumber. Terrified, I came out in the gallery and peeked down from the railing. No suspicious movement could be seen.

I went back in and got dressed. I stepped down from the back of the building with much caution and discreetly scanned the road outside. Even though no one could be seen on the road when I stepped out to report the incident at a police station, my courage failed me and I returned home quietly. While in the gallery, I dialled the same number from which the threatening call had come. It continued to ring but no one picked the phone. I tried calling five or six times, but there was no response. Then I dialled Mandar's number. I wanted to forewarn him to stay alert and tell him about the call. Mandar told me he had received a similar call at around 12.40 a.m., ten minutes after I got it. We received calls from different numbers, but from the same area.

Mandar said he hurled back abuses at the caller. Later on, the caller threatened Mandar, 'You guys chant Telgi Telgi all day. Now we will shove Telgi up your ass ... We will kill you. Your days are over. See, what all we can do. You guys have no clue who you are messing with.'

It is another thing that Mandar responded in their own language. But unlike me, he was neither scared nor shaken. He said, 'If anyone comes to my house, I will beat them black and blue.' Mandar had a short fuse. If he had had a little more aggression, he would have been apt for the police force. I still cautioned him to stay alert.

I quietly entered home after finishing the phone call and closed the door. Wanting to safeguard my family from any possible danger, I closed the window tightly and checked the back door again, before retiring to bed. The conversation with Mandar offered some comfort to my troubled mind, but I was still shaken. My one-year-old daughter sleeping next to me turned in her sleep and gurgled. I looked at her innocent expression. She had a serenity on her face. I thought about what her future would be like, should something happen to me. The family's apprehensions were legitimate. I spent the whole night tossing and turning. I could barely catch on sleep and woke up many times at the slightest movement.

Next morning, I got ready and headed to the Gamdevi police station to register my complaint. I was assigned complaint number CR No. 1337/03, after which I proceeded to office. I informed my resident editor Srinivas Jain and head of Hindi news Abhigyan Prakash of the incident. They heard me out in a semi-awake state but never ever discussed the matter with me. I informed the Delhi head office about the threat and emailed the managing editor Rajdeep Sardesai, the head of the Hindi channel Dibang, and NDTV all in all, Prannoy Roy and Radhika Roy. Everyone suggested I exercise caution and stay alert. The company suggested that I opt for police protection since we all suspected the involvement of a disgruntled policeman behind this threat. Everyone at NDTV became extremely concerned about my safety.

Mandar also registered a police complaint at MIDC police station. The investigation revealed that the calls had been made from two public calling booths in Thane. This meant there was no chance of nabbing the culprit.

I spoke to Star News correspondent Jitendra Dixit. He said he had also received a threatening call a few days back, but it had had no connection with the Telgi case.

The next day, all newspapers prominently printed the news about the threatening calls that Mandar and I had received. *Navbharat Times* went on to state that 'Sanjay Singh's exclusive report was instrumental in shaking the foundation of R.S. Sharma's Mumbai Commissioner's seat'.

The next day, state home minister Kripa Shankar Singh and I met. He proposed police protection, which I refused. He informed me that Chief Minister Sushilkumar Shinde had instructed him to talk to me. The chief minister had been occupied with the Madhya Pradesh election campaign in rural areas and thus was unable to talk to me directly.

The same suggestion came from deputy chief minister and home minister Chhagan Bhujbal's office. I had valid reasons to not accept police protection:

1. My reporting on the Telgi case had been most detrimental for the police. Seeking protection from the same police force in this scenario was absurd.
2. Secondly, having police with me all the time would mean giving the GPS of my life in their hands. Their consistent shadowing would deprive me of many an exclusive news and may even expose the identity of my precious sources.
3. I lived in a 200 square foot house with my wife, daughter and parents. The house could barely contain my family. Deputing security outside the house wouldn't have been appropriate. I used my dilapidated motorcycle for my daily commute. Imagining a security person riding pillion on my old bike would only make me a laughing stock.

But somewhere, we had a feeling that this was an empty threat, with a bleak probability of any execution being planned.

In the end, it was decided that we would leave for an unknown destination for a few days to avoid any kind of mishappening. We took fifteen days' leave from office. The idea was to return to Mumbai after the threat died down. Third day since the threat had been made, late in the night, Mandar and I, along with two of our colleagues, left Mumbai without informing anyone about our intended destination. Our abode for the next ten days were pristine natural locations in Madhya Pradesh, such as Pachmarhi, Kanha National Park, Bhedaghat and Khajuraho.

Before leaving, during a conversation with a senior officer of the SIT, I shared in a lighter tone how I had put my plans for a holiday on hold, anticipating Sharma's arrest. He asked me to proceed with a free mind and have a great time.

We did doubt if Sharma's arrest would happen so soon, but in life, things never happen the way you want.

25

Commissioner Sharma's Exit and Arrest

1 December 2003

Monday

People realized post Wagal's arrest that even IPS officers weren't beyond the reach of the law.

A double-edged sword hung over Sharma. On one side, he risked losing his post, and on the other, he faced the danger of action by the SIT.

Sharma had caused tremendous embarrassment to the government. His biggest protector, Bhujbal, chose to keep his lips sealed over the Sharma issue. The Bombay High Court instructed SIT chief S.S. Puri to investigate

Commissioner Sharma's Exit and Arrest

Sharma's role in the scam, as he had raised questions on the credibility of the Jaiswal Report.

S.S. Puri summoned R.S. Sharma to the SIT office multiple times for questioning. He also found there had been lapses on Sharma's part in the investigation into the scam, post which it became tougher for Sharma to defend himself. Before, during and after the investigation, Sharma kept convincing the media of his innocence. He declared himself untainted and refuted all charges levelled against him.

But it became difficult for the government to retain Sharma at the prestigious post of Mumbai police commissioner. At last, they decided to remove him and transfer him to the DGP office as additional director general (administration). Sharma was due for retirement on 30 November. Removing him from the post of commissioner two weeks before his retirement was a matter of great disgrace for him. After a few days, Sharma was again transferred to an even lower post at the insignificant state transport department—one of much less importance than his previous portfolios. Sharma did not take charge of the new position until the end.

Sharma retired on 30 November and within twenty-four hours of his retirement, was arrested by the SIT on 1 December.

The irony was that we left for our holiday on the day of Sharma's arrest. We were at a tribal village in Chhindwara district, Madhya Pradesh, thousand kilometres away from

Mumbai, when the news of Sharma's arrest reached us. We watched it on Doordarshan. Actually, we had no inkling that Sharma would be arrested so soon, else we wouldn't have left Mumbai at all. We suspected the SIT was waiting for Sharma to retire. They didn't want to see one of their own senior IPS officers fall from grace while still in service.

Some of the allegations made against Sharma were as follows:

1. Karnataka Police had taped the conversation between Telgi and Pune's ACP Mulani, in which Mulani demanded a bribe. Sharma was informed of the same. Besides this, Sharma was well versed with the poor track records of ACP Mulani with regard to corruption. Sharma did not remove ACP Mulani from the investigating team even after being informed that Mulani had demanded a bribe. He was not only retained in the investigation team thereafter, but also sent to Bangalore more than once, which included a private meeting with Telgi. Not even an investigation officer was sent along with them.

2. In October 2002, Pune's then additional commissioner Mushrif brought to Sharma's notice the inclusion and deletion of certain names from the chargesheet and the ones without a rational correlation with evidence on record having been shown as accused. As per Mushrif, this was all done

with mala fide intentions. Yet Sharma failed to discipline SP Mulani, ensuring Telgi continued to receive ACP Mulani's assistance in his scam.

3. Application of MCOCA on the stamp scam was delayed. The investigation officer scuttled a proposal to apply the provisions of MCOCA on 9 July 2002, but the chargesheet was filed on 3 September 2002. Despite having all the rights, Sharma failed to ensure timely application of MCOCA.

4. DIG Subodh Jaiswal and additional DGP Sri Kumar, top officers of the SIT in Maharashtra and Karnataka, respectively, personally briefed Sharma about Telgi enjoying the comforts of his home at Cuffe Parade in Mumbai, after they raided the place on 9 January 2003. It happened when R.S. Sharma was the police commissioner of Mumbai. No active steps were taken by Sharma to ensure the immediate suspension though it was within his powers to do it with immediate effect. Suspension was done after a delay of five days. Despite possession of powers which he could have used against the erring officers, he protected and projected Kamath as a good and responsible officer.

5. Telgi's business was going on even when he was in the custody of Mumbai Police and Sharma was the police commissioner of Mumbai.

Sharma was brought before the court in Pune the police commissioner day after his arrest. He was the Police Commissioner of Pune until a year ago. Not only the court premises but the road outside the court was swarming with people.

In the courtroom, R.S. Sharma said he was being 'singled out' and being treated unfairly by the SIT. Sharma claimed he had an 'unblemished record' of thirty-five years in the police department. He added, 'Those responsible for helping the Telgi syndicate have been left out and I have been pinned down in this case.' He said the SIT had charged him for the same lapses which had been mentioned in the government chargesheet served to him during the departmental inquiry. Hence, this amounted to 'double jeopardy'.

A well-armed public prosecutor, Raja Thakare, said, 'We will have to investigate whether Sharma was under political pressure to give patronage to Telgi and, if so, who are the politicians involved.' He added that Sharma knew quite well what Telgi was doing.

Sharma refuted all allegations against him. Later, he even maintained that applying MCOCA on Telgi and other accused was inappropriate. Sharma was sent into police custody by the court. After the court proceedings were over, Sharma was rushed into lockup.

After a few months, R.S. Sharma was granted bail and years later, he was discharged.

Holidays Over, Back to Mumbai

Post our holiday, we were back in Mumbai. I celebrated my second wedding anniversary on 9 December and joined the office on 10 December. Much happened in Mumbai during our absence and I regret not being part of it. But the media and police in Mumbai were cooking up another story: they thought we went missing on purpose, on a secret mission. We tried our best to explain our absence, but no one believed our version of the story.

In between, the state's former DGP Subash Malhotra was questioned as well. Media also speculated about former IG T.K. Chowdhary's involvement, but nothing came out, as was anticipated. Because of this, rumours were rife that the SIT was only targeting a select few, affiliated to specific groups. There was still some time before the next big arrest would be made, perhaps next year. Although any arrest post R.S. Sharma's may seem minuscule, but DCP Pradeep Sawant held a position of command in the department.

26

The Arrest of the King of Encounters

9 January 2004

Pradeep Sawant was a much-celebrated DCP in Mumbai Police. At first, he tried to avoid investigation into the Telgi scam case altogether, then reluctantly scraped through two rounds of questioning. Three of his reportees and two of his superiors had already been arrested. He was caught in the middle, but still going scot-free. Policemen from his coterie were spreading the untruth that the SIT had given a clean chit to Sawant in this matter.

But the beginning of 2004 cleared all misunderstandings.

Sawant was called in for investigation to the SIT office on 9 January 2004. After thorough questioning, he was shown an old NDTV report. The SIT had been unsatisfied with Sawant's responses. During the interrogation, Sawant told the SIT that there was no connection between finding Telgi at home during custody in January 2003, and the seizure of fake stamps worth 830 crore rupees from Bhiwandi a few days after.

But during the interview given to TV media on 16 April 2003, Sawant had said that both matters were related. NDTV had aired the said interview and it became crucial evidence against Sawant, catalysing his arrest.

Sawant had dug his own grave in that interview. We telecast the news at 8.45 p.m.: 'Sawant has been arrested'—but came to know later that he was arrested an hour after we broke the news. Sawant's questioning was still on then. Sachin Vaze continued to dismiss the news of Sawant's arrest. Despite all news channels airing the news, he kept refuting it as a rumour.

Allegations levelled against Sawant were as follows:

1. All the charges levelled against his boss, Sridhar Wagal, were repeated for DCP Sawant. His conduct was similar to Wagal's in that he had deliberately not taken action, granted Inspector Kamath free will, transferred balance cases to Kamath, etc. Sawant was also charged with having conspired to commit,

abet and knowingly facilitate the commission of an organized crime, namely, the printing and sale of fake stamp papers, and thereby was guilty of offences under MCOCA, which carried a minimum punishment of five years' imprisonment, but which could also be extended to a life term.

2. As per the supplementary chargesheet, Sawant was charged with rendering help and support on his own, in the commission of an organized crime by Telgi's crime syndicate, by abstaining from taking necessary action by himself and through his subordinate officers. He had directed his subordinates that Telgi should not be kept in the lockup. This had facilitated the continuance of illegal activity by Telgi, including the disposal of his ill-gotten properties, while he was in police custody. Telgi was also accorded special treatment by Sawant.

Sawant's lawyers continued to maintain that the case was based on fragmentary evidence. The kind of acrimonious reactions Sawant's arrest attracted had not been felt during other arrests. Newspapers cited Sawant's earlier work credits—Shiv Sena's mouthpiece *Saamna* was at the forefront, defending Sawant. *Saamna* wrote how his arrest was the result of groupism in the police force. The SIT's work was met with criticism in *Saamna*. In his statement,

Shiv Sena supremo Bal Thackeray also declared Sawant's arrest unnecessary. After more than a year, Sawant was granted bail. After more than three years, a special MCOCA court discharged Pradeep Sawant, R.S. Sharma and Vasisth Andhale. Five years after his arrest, Sawant was reinstated.

27

Fall of Bhujbal

28 February 2004

Saturday

Chhagan Bhujbal always had the image of a combatant leader. He moved to the Congress after dedicating twenty years of his political career to the Shiv Sena. In the 1995 elections, Congress lost and even Bhujbal lost ignominiously to a rookie candidate from the Shiv Sena. For once, it looked like his political career was over, but his reverence of Sharad Pawar came in handy and he was able to make a backdoor entry into the corridors of politics as a legislative council member. Sharad Pawar even appointed him as the leader of the opposition. It was Bhujbal who single-handedly held the opposition's spine straight and

Fall of Bhujbal

put up a tough fight against the Shiv Sena–BJP government in power.

In 1999, after Sharad Pawar left the Congress to form the NCP, Bhujbal too moved out with Pawar. In the elections that year, Congress–NCP formed a coalition government. Ignoring all the Maratha stalwarts from western Maharashtra, Sharad Pawar made Bhujbal, from the other backward class (OBC), the deputy chief minister of the state. Barring Bhujbal, no other minister of that government had a close tryst with controversy. But Bhujbal and controversies were in a mutual admiration club. In spite of tremendous efforts, the opposition failed to beset Bhujbal. But the Telgi case initiated Bhujbal's fall.

Bhujbal was the home minister and so the police department fell within his ambit. The rot in the same police department had now become the talk of the town.

He left no stone unturned to defend R.S. Sharma and the corrupt officials of the Mumbai Crime Branch, who were neck-deep in the Telgi scam case, in front of the media. The opposition's strategy was to trap Bhujbal using the name of Antim Totla. Antim Totla was considered a close NCP aide of Bhujbal's and his name had found mention in Telgi-related cases.

The opposition made the final onslaught on Bhujbal with all their might. At the ongoing December 2003 winter assembly session in Nagpur, the opposition surrounded Bhujbal from all sides. No one from his party, NCP or coalition ally Congress, came to his rescue. The opposition created a furore in the assembly over a letter from the arrested police officer Dilip Kamath made public, which hinted at Telgi prospering under Bhujbal's directive. Bhujbal's nephew Sameer's name, too, got dragged into the controversy. Bhujbal's resignation from the post of deputy chief minister was demanded by all sides, but despite being in the firing range, he tried to stand his ground.

On 19 December 2003, Telgi's lawyer in Bangalore accused Bhujbal of being connected to the Telgi scam. Later, Telgi invalidated his lawyer's allegations.

Bhujbal was hospitalized for a few days and once out, clarified that he was neither leaving his position nor was he being asked to do so.

After Bhujbal's statement, journalists thought he had again got away with it, but something else was destined to happen. Bhujbal was looking for a dignified way to exit. Suddenly, one day, 23 December 2003, NCP workers vandalized the Zee TV Mumbai office. The pretext for this was the distasteful remarks about Bhujbal made during a programme aired on the Alpha Marathi channel of Zee News. By the evening, Bhujbal resigned, owning the moral responsibility for the attack on the media by NCP workers.

Everyone knows what happened. Bhujbal made much hue and cry on resigning over moral grounds but it was evident that in politics, two plus two was not always four. A vow of morality in those times, and that too by politicians, was indeed hard to swallow. The second most powerful man in the state government relinquishing his power that easily? How was one supposed to believe the unthinkable that easily?

The crux of the matter was timing. Telgi underwent scientific tests like the narco analysis and lie-detector tests. The purpose of these was to bring the truth to the forefront. Rumours were rife that the day of the arrival of the test reports and Bhujbal's resignation coinciding and being unrelated was too implausible.

After two days, Bhujbal was again hospitalized and one day, suddenly, he left for Kerala for further treatment. In my eight years of journalistic life, this was the first time I watched Bhujbal lose his composure. The man who had faced the media with grit during his toughest battles was suddenly shying away from the media. Some called it desertion, but journalists knew the matter must have been grave, or else Bhujbal would never have behaved like this.

The fog started to clear up slowly. The SIT sent summons to Bhujbal's nephew Sameer for questioning in the first week of January. Sameer wasn't in Mumbai, but overseas. The SIT moved the dates thrice, but each time, he gave the excuse of being overseas.

Amidst all this, on 17 January, Bhujbal returned to Mumbai and called for a press conference. He made many controversial statements during the press conference, some of which were:

- The SIT wanted to persecute him and his family by using all the tricks of the trade, with or without evidence. This was why his near and dear ones were being harassed.

- The SIT had lost its way and instead of investigating the Telgi stamp scam, they had got busy settling scores with their competitors within the police department.
- The SIT investigations were having an adverse impact on the morale of police personnel.
- The actions taken so far had been driven by revenge as the DIG of the SIT, Subodh Jaiswal, was upset with Bhujbal.
- The SIT investigations were targeting selective people. The SIT was planning action against Bhujbal, but was deliberately not questioning politicians of the opposition parties. The roots of this case were widespread, leading to politicians in Delhi.
- The SIT was purposely leaking news about Bhujbal to the media. Before Sameer Bhujbal got summoned for questioning, the media got the news. Shiv Sena leader and former chief minister Narayan Rane was questioned as well, but not a word got out.
- The underworld crime syndicates stood to benefit from the arrest of police officials of the Mumbai Police Crime Branch which worked against them. The Crime Branch, who relentlessly fought underworld crime, was highly demotivated and dejected at the moment.

- Sameer Bhujbal had no connections with the Telgi stamp scam, so why was he being troubled? The questions needed to be directed at himself, not his nephew.

Chhagan Bhujbal said he was ready to face the SIT in the investigations. Journalists tried to corner Bhujbal on the following two questions:

- Bhujbal had praised the investigation work conducted by the SIT earlier. When he was the deputy chief minister, he had said nothing adverse about the SIT. But why did he decide to become vocal when Sameer Bhujbal's name was dragged into the case? Why did he not raise his objections earlier?
- The other day, Bhujbal's arch-rival Shiv Sena supremo Bal Thackeray also called the investigations done by the SIT wrong in the party's mouthpiece *Saamna*. Was that a mere coincidence?

I asked two more questions from my side:

- Was Bhujbal wary of his and Sameer's arrest?
- Would he be applying for anticipatory bail?

Bhujbal dragged the answer to the first question and circumvented it. He responded with a 'No' to the second question.

If one was to summarize the points raised by Bhujbal and his body language, his expressions gave away the anxiety haunting his mind, of probably falling into the hands of the SIT for the investigation.

A pleasant moment for me arrived in the form of Bhujbal being cordial and friendly towards me, when we met alone later on. He inquired after my well-being, while informally interacting with all the other journalists en masse before the press conference. His friendly demeanour took me by surprise as I was anticipating hostility and seething anger from him.

28
The Nephew in a Corner

I wasn't well acquainted with Sameer Bhujbal, but knew Pankaj Bhujbal adequately well. Sameer was Chhagan Bhujbal's nephew, while Pankaj was his son. Whenever we met socially, we always greeted each other. I had met Sameer and Pankaj during the party for the movie *Kagaar*. After the usual discussion on politics, the Telgi scam came up, so we discussed the case.

Then, I met Sameer over a meal at Chhagan Bhujbal's official bungalow in Ramtek. This was followed by multiple telephone conversations. He shared that neither he nor Chhagan Bhujbal had any role to play in the Telgi stamp scam. He alleged that his name had unnecessarily been dragged into the police's internal factional war—the opposition duo of BJP–Shiv Sena was targeting Bhujbal. He said that policemen misled and continuously gave wrong briefings to Bhujbal. Sameer also shared that Chhagan had had no contribution to giving a clean chit to R.S. Sharma.

I also affirmed that through its narrative, the police may have misled Bhujbal, which entrapped him in the controversy. I also told Sameer that they had voluntarily chosen to make the policemen their eyes, ears and nose. I shared with him that the current buzz amongst journalists was that Bhujbal may land into trouble due to his favouring of policemen. Sameer clarified that he had no relation to his uncle's official and political work. His hands were full with his educational institution's work.

The SIT had already interrogated Chhagan Bhujbal's secretary, Sanjay Bankar, for six hours in January and next in line was Sameer.

On 19 January 2004, Sameer was scheduled to appear for questioning before the SIT. Sameer reached their office with a bevy of supporters and the police had a hard time controlling them. Sameer's interrogation lasted for about five hours. His supporters looked troubled the whole time. Anticipating arrest, every supporter was asking the same question: Was the SIT's white Qualis visible outside the office? Until now, all those arrested had been taken to Pune in a White Qualis.

When I reached a nearby hotel to have tea in the afternoon, I met Sachin Ahir (nephew of underworld don Arun Gawli), along with his supporters. Sachin Ahir became a minister later and also produced a few movies. Ahir was an NCP MLA and was considered to have been close to Bhujbal. I had known him for a long time. Over tea, the discussion ensued and he asked, 'What do you think?'

'What do I think about what?' I asked.

'You tell,' he asked.

'You tell,' I repeated.

'You know about everything,' he said.

'Not everything. But I do keep an eye on a few things. It is the nature of my work,' I answered.

'What do you think? Will the Qualis show up?' The MLA felt the terror of the Qualis too.

'It's not visible yet.' I paused and then said further, 'Perhaps it may not show up at all.'

This brought a smile to his face. Ahir said, 'If you say so, it must be right.'

I could not gauge whether this was a question or a compliment. Anyway, Mandar and I finished our tea and returned to the SIT office.

By the evening, I got information that the questioning had concluded and Sameer would be on his way home shortly.

After some time, I got a call from Jitendra Awhad. (The credit for organizing the fantastic dahi–handi celebrations, which won international recognition, goes to Jitendra Awhad. Sharad Pawar's favourite, Awhad was also appointed cabinet minister later.) He was an MLA, head of the NCP's youth wing, and a close confidant of Bhujbal's back then.

'Have I heard right?' Awhad asked me.

'How would I know what you heard?' I responded.

'That he is coming out.' Now I understood what he meant.

'Yes.'

He asked, 'Is it confirmed?'

'Yes, we are running the news,' I told him.

'Should I tell his uncle?' he asked again.

'Go ahead,' I replied.

'If you are so sure, it must be true.' Saying this, he disconnected the phone.

The news spread like wildfire within Sameer's group of supporters. Their tired and despondent faces lit up. It felt like a close shave.

Sameer stepped out after some time and left for home in his car. Journalists chased him and reached the Ramtek bungalow. After some time, Sameer and Chhagan Bhujbal met the journalists and answered their questions. Sameer had a tilak on his forehead as if he had just returned after winning a war. There was dew-like freshness on the faces of both uncle and nephew. They were responding to the journalists in a jolly good mood. Sameer said it had been a light inquiry and there was not much to say.

After a few days, Sameer was called in for another round of interrogation.

Wednesday, 25 February 2004, was the day of Sameer's follow-up inquiry. Keeping last time's experience in mind, a large number of police personnel were deputed to avert any untoward legal complications that may arise

The Nephew in a Corner

due to Sameer's supporters. The supporters were halted a kilometre before the SIT office. Sameer Bhujbal came without any pomp and show. The inquiry lasted for more than five hours.

I wanted to cover the news, but despite my request, another reporter was sent over. It had happened many times in the past as well that I was removed from the coverage of a big news item just because I was a Hindi-speaking reporter. I was usually replaced by a 'bilingual' reporter. It was seen as an advantage since such a reporter could transmit news through a 'live chat', that is, direct telecast of the situation in both Hindi and English simultaneously. Meanwhile, the other (Hindi) reporter would work on another news. This also helped in mitigating the shortage of reporters—an economical solution. A product of the Hindi-medium education system, I understood English, but did not possess the verbal proficiency levels needed to cover news for a good-quality English TV channel.

Bilingual reporters are (mostly) English-speaking reporters, who somehow manage to cover Hindi news. The proficiency levels in Hindi don't apply to English-speaking bilingual reporters. They can easily get away with using insipid, broken, barely passable, lifeless Hindi laced with English words, in their reporting.

A bilingual reporter is the distinct need for and a by-product of dynamism of journalism. Many senior reporters foresee the bright prospects for a bilingual reporter in the news industry, and I would be hardly surprised if their wish came true in the future. Hindi journalists like me have our own limitations. To attain the high proficiency levels of English that one needs to find acceptance on English channels is a tough task. And just improving language skills doesn't suffice: diction and delivery are equally important. But my sincere advice to Hindi journalists entering the world of journalism is to start paying attention to this trend.

Not only in journalism, Hindi language can be seen struggling for survival in all fields of life.

29

Bhujbal's Slipper

28 February 2004

Saturday

The day when Sameer Bhujbal was called for an interrogation for the third time was upon us. Sameer reached the SIT office at 11 a.m. and the interrogation ended at 2 p.m. As it had happened previously, Sameer did not interact with the media outside the SIT office. Like the last two times, the media headed straight to Bhujbal's house in Ramtek. As always, Bhujbal's house was thronging with supporters.

The large hall delegated for press interaction also had sixty or seventy of his supporters present. Almost all electronic media was present there. Along with NDTV, Star News, Aaj Tak, Sahara Samay, Zee News, In Mumbai, C-News reporters, a few journalists from print media were present as well. We were informed that media interaction would begin at 4 p.m.

But at a quarter to four, Sameer appeared to meet the media. He came alone. Unlike what we expected, Chhagan Bhujbal did not join him. The press conference started. Some questions were asked. These were the same as last time, and Sameer gave the same replies:

Question: What were you asked?

Sameer: There were a few questions remaining from the last time, those were asked.

Question: What were those questions? Can you please elaborate?

Sameer: I cannot share what the questions were. Whatever they asked of me, I responded.

Question: Have they asked you to come back?

Sameer: I don't know. They haven't said anything yet.

Question: Were you asked about receiving money from Telgi directly or indirectly?

Sameer: No.

I had asked the last question and Sameer left the hall after responding.

The media too had nothing more to ask. But the last question asked was destined to cause commotion in the near future. Bhujbal's supporters continued to chant slogans supporting Sameer as we exited.

Bhujbal's Slipper

The journalists were about to leave when Chhagan Bhujbal arrived. He sat on a chair in front of the mics. We had no need to interview him at that point of time, but since Bhujbal was already there, it would be more appropriate to ask him some questions out of courtesy. It is pertinent to mention how Bhujbal had always been media-friendly and was always granting interviews, never disappointing the media fraternity.

Bhujbal widened his eyes and said in a light vein, 'And start now, who is the leader here? Start questioning.'

I spoke from behind the camera. 'Sir, everyone is a leader here. We can start from anywhere.'

Bhujbal looked at me and said, 'Of course, you are the ringleader and your word carries a lot of weight. You start.'

What had started as a friendly banter was meandering into complex questioning.

First, three generic questions were asked, like 'What was Sameer asked?' 'You are scheduled for questioning next week. Are you ready?' etc.

Then, I raised a question, 'Bhujbal sir, Sameer was probably asked this question and you may be asked as well. Have you ever received any money from Telgi, directly or indirectly? Would you like to share any comments or offer any clarification on this?'

The question was serious. But I took utmost care to keep to etiquette, choose my language and words carefully and remember my limits before raising it.

Bhujbal vociferously denied ever taking any money from Telgi. He also staked his claim to being the one who exposed the scam and spoiled Telgi's party in the first place. But in the last thirty seconds of his response, Bhujbal roared, his face hardening with anger. 'I did not take any money. What kind of questions do you guys ask? It is as if you were writing a caption. "Was Bhujbal given any money?" If anyone asks me such ridiculous questions now, I will take off my slipper! No one wants to face my wrath if my patience ends!'

By the end of the last sentence, his voice had started quivering and his language was all over the place. He made his last statement, looking me right in the eye.

There was pin-drop silence in the room. All journalists were in a state of shock. Coming straight to his point in such anger was not anticipated. There were fifty or sixty supporters of Bhujbal present in that room then, and many more were outside. The supporters flashed me a death stare. I was sure I would get a solid thrashing any minute. My fear was natural, considering the way Bhujbal had roared at me. I started sweating profusely in the air-conditioned room. I wiped the sweat on my forehead and looked at my fellow reporters. Every eye I met was silently cursing me for landing them in a soup along with myself.

The reporter for Aaj Tak, Sahil Joshi, broke this temporary trance and asked the next question. Two or three more questions were asked, giving Bhujbal room to put forward his point of view and control the situation. The agitated Bhujbal soon got up and left the room. The supporters raised adrenaline-fuelled slogans as he departed.

I rushed out. First and foremost, I took the recorded tape from our cameraman and ran towards the spot where our OB van was stationed. Fearing violence breaking out against me, I wanted to leave the place as soon as possible. In the past, I had been assaulted four or five times in my career as a journalist. During the Gujarat riots coverage, I almost lost my life. It wasn't a new experience for me, but who would ever want a solid thrashing? An agitated crowd's fury knows no remorse nor fear, and God alone knows how every human being is scared of being beaten black and blue.

In the meantime, I overheard four supporters of Bhujbal's asking the Sahara Samay reporter Prabhat Kathe if I was the reporter Chhagan Bhujbal had referred to in his comment. Prabhat Kathe misled them, saying it was someone else and not me. Later, Prabhat Kathe told me a few Bhujbal supporters were on a lookout to assault me. NDTV's OB van was parked about fifty metres from Bhujbal's house. I took long steps to reach there. As a few supporters threw angry glances at me, I increased my pace. Handing over the cassette to the OB van operator, I asked him to uplink it immediately and meet me at the office later, along with the tape.

After saying this, I jumped into the other office car and rushed out of the place. I heaved a sigh of relief once I was out of the danger zone. At least the danger had been averted for now. The office was forty minutes away. I kept pondering over Bhujbal's unprecedented reaction and threat. The same question was posed to Sameer, but he had answered it so peacefully. Then what had made a seasoned politician like Bhujbal lose his composure and act so recklessly?

Owning the moral responsibility for the attack on the media by his supporters through the vandalizing of the office of Zee TV only a month and a half ago, Bhujbal had resigned from the post of deputy chief minister and home minister. Bhujbal had used the attack on the fourth pillar of democracy as moral grounds to add credibility to his resignation.

The Shiv Sena was the only party which had resorted to violence and vandalism while dealing with journalists in the past. It is important to remember Bhujbal's long association with the Shiv Sena since his advent into politics, at this juncture. Though in the last twelve years Bhujbal had always raised his voice against any attack on the journalists by the Shiv Sena, yet the same man had lost his cool today in this manner. There was nothing wrong, really, with the question that had elicited such a volatile outburst.

The last two or three months had been detrimental for reporters' well-being. NCP supporters had vandalized the Zee News office and, more recently, Sahara News reporters had also been thrashed mercilessly by the Bahujan Samaj Party (BSP) supporters during a rally organized by Mayawati at Shivaji Park in Mumbai. A reporter had been murdered in Vidarbha, and now, Bhujbal's slipper!

That slipper had my name inscribed on its sole and my head had been identified as its intended recipient. I had been losing hair, but I was in no rush to go completely bald, so soon. My fear had subsided by the time I reached office, but the fear of Bhujbal's supporters attacking the office still loomed large. I shared this incident with my editors, edited the news and uplinked it to Delhi.

Headlines of 7 p.m. news—all channels were on a shouting spree, flashing visuals of Bhujbal's angry outburst. His threat to hit journalists with slippers continued to play on loop all night.

I had forwarded all my mobile calls to the office landline, as the editing room I was working in had low mobile connectivity. I was later told that they had received at least ten calls from Bhujbal's home and his secretary, asking for me.

I thought there were only two possibilities—either they wanted to threaten me further, or they wanted to apologize upon realizing their mistake. It happens sometimes that in the heat of the moment people say things they have no intention to act on. A third possibility was they might request me to stop the story from being aired, expecting which, frankly, would have been a foolish proposition.

Anyway, I thought they would call again if there was anything urgent, but no call came after the 7 p.m. news went on air.

Later, many journalists from the fraternity called me. Everyone assured me of their solidarity. They all advised me to stay alert and take care of myself.

Around midnight, I left the office. Fear rode pillion with me on my journey back home. I wore a helmet while driving my motorcycle, which shielded my identity. From afar, I spotted a few unknown faces under my building. Anticipating danger, I drove past them and then took another round. When I felt that my fear was unsubstantiated, I decided to enter the building. After the third round, when I reached the building, those people were gone. I heaved a sigh of relief.

Various thoughts were floating in my mind as I retired for the night after dinner. I was musing over how the anticipation of violence was more frightening than the act of violence itself. The people standing under my building were probably innocent bystanders, but the fear rooted deep within my heart made me speculate over their motives and fear their appearance. Though I believe every person in the universe is scared of something or the other, the one who can channel his internal strength to conquer his fear and continue working is the bravest of all. Sleep soon quietened my thoughts.

I woke up the next morning and saw that the *Times of India*, *Mid-Day*, *Lok Satta*, *Saamna*, *Maharashtra Times*, *Sakaal*, *Lokmat*, *The Asian Age*, and almost all other newspapers had covered the news. Some newspapers had even quoted my name. The ever-image-conscious Chhagan Bhujbal would have despised the weekend edition of newspapers that Sunday.

The most surprising thing of all was that my own family had missed watching the news on TV last night. So in the morning, when the newspapers arrived, what followed was the same old discussion. Each member of the family counselled me by turns to let go of my shenanigans. Why was I unnecessarily insisting on covering Telgi-related news? What if something happened to me? I had had enough of this in the past. I also knew there was a reason God gave us two ears. If they were meant only for listening, then one ear was enough!

But one thing was certain: hereon, I needed to watch my back. This was no ordinary incident. One by one, I had earned the animosity of many within the power circles. From policemen to politicians, I had upset them all.

After two days, Sameer Bhujbal's PA, Shahu, called me on my mobile. 'Sanjay Singh, Bhau will talk.' Sameer was often addressed as 'Bhau' by his close associates.

'Yes, this is Sameer speaking,' Sameer came on the line.

'Yes, Sameer ji. Please tell me.' I greeted him. 'How are you?'

Sameer laughed. The laughter indicated that he was wondering where to begin. 'I am all right. How have you been?'

'What can I say? Thanks to you, I am getting enough publicity.' I was referring to the newspaper reports.

Sameer laughed again. 'Because of saheb, not me.' By saheb he meant Chhagan Bhujbal.

'One and the same thing. For me, you both are the same,' I said.

'There has been a misunderstanding.' He cleared his throat. 'Saheb wasn't singling you out. He just said it generally.'

I replied, 'If any man watches Bhujbal saheb's interview on TV, he would clearly see saheb's anger being directed at me. Some supporters were also looking for me later.'

'No, no, there is nothing like that. Don't read too much into it. Saheb wasn't targeting you at all. You see, we are highly stressed right now. Saheb is under so much pressure. All of you, please try to understand our situation.'

Sameer said all of it to demonstrate remorse over the slipper incident. After a day or two, Bhujbal again clarified that the slipper statement was not aimed at journalists.

The time to question Chhagan Bhujbal post the interrogation of Sameer Bhujbal was fast approaching. The SIT wanted to schedule Bhujbal's inquiry for 1 March but he had a defamation case hearing lined up for that day in the court. Next day, on 2 March, was Muharram, which limited the feasibility of police arrangement outside the SIT office. The crowd of supporters anticipated during Bhujbal's investigation thus made 2 March unsuitable for the inquiry.

The news came later that date was unconfirmed.

4 March is my birthday. By the afternoon, information of Chhagan Bhujbal's questioning at an undisclosed location and not at the SIT's Worli office, came in. Later, I got a tip that his inquiry was being conducted at the SRP

compound in the Jogeshwari suburb. Since the news was yet unconfirmed, it didn't feel safe to play it on air. But slowly, word got out. Most of the media lined up outside the SRP complex. No one was allowed to step in. All reporters waited patiently for hours outside the gate, by the highway. The news was confirmed at seven in the evening, and soon the same headline was running on every news channel: 'SIT questioned Chhagan Bhujbal'.

Then came in the information that the inquiry was being held for the past two days. The whole media was reeling from this revelation.

The inquiry conducted on 3 and 4 March had been a highly guarded affair. This was 'special treatment' for Chhagan Bhujbal. Chhagan Bhujbal always maintained that he was harassed in the name of inquiry. Some leaders of the opposition, such as Narayan Rane of the Shiv Sena, were questioned too, but the SIT had kept it confidential. Bhujbal claimed he was singled out when his turn came, and that the SIT tried to humiliate him publicly through the media.

Bhujbal's accusations followed by his aggravated reactions made many believe that the SIT had crumbled under the pressure and made Bhujbal's inquiry classified. But I can't fathom to date how that could have benefited anyone. Because news like this is difficult to contain. One way or another it comes out and then it gets published, as it is meant to be. Then why the charade? Many journalists like myself were thinking along these lines. They later said that the venue change was done to avert any possible law and order situation which may have arisen due to the large gathering of Bhujbal's supporters expected outside the SIT's Worli office. But these were ludicrous arguments. Should the law change its course just because a politician could exercise his power over the masses and cause disruption to its functioning? Just because the said leader's party was ruling the government?

If the SIT was so empathetic over his public image distortion, then why its stepmotherly treatment towards the others? People like R.S. Sharma, Pradeep Sawant, Ashok Basak (former additional chief secretary) had also been called in for questioning. Not only that, some were called more than once. Several were arrested. Only statements were recorded for a few; but if one was to go by Bhujbal's logic, even this much was enough for all of them to lose face in the public. Then why discriminate between him and the others? Everyone must be considered innocent until proven guilty.

This pretext of calling Bhujbal separately to avoid clashing with his crowd of supporters made no logical sense whatsoever. The media was not upset just because of missed 'news'. Everyone was questioning the intent behind the unusual action. It was the first time the media cast doubts on the SIT's conduct.

Bhujbal did address the media later, and responded to their queries. Bhujbal shared that he had cooperated with the SIT, answered all their questions and made all the requisite information available. But once again, Bhujbal raised a question against the SIT's direction of questioning. Bhujbal told journalists that the SIT was concentrating only on scam cases related to Pune's Bund Garden police station, whereas scams needed a broader investigation on a larger scale.

30

Satyapal's and Parambir's 'Inquiries'

I got the news that Mumbai Police joint commissioner (crime) Satyapal Singh (who later became Mumbai's police commissioner, then two-time BJP member of Parliament, and a cabinet minister in the BJP-led central government) was questioned in the Telgi case. This information came to me at 9 p.m. Saturday night current affairs programmes had already been aired. I thought, 'If I share this news now, it will be telecast only at midnight.' This would mean it would not get the attention it deserved, so I decided to hold on to it until the next day. Next day, on Sunday, we broke the news. Other channels also relayed it. News needs to be balanced, so I dialled Satyapal Singh's number but his mobile kept ringing and was unanswered. I gave up after a few attempts but resolved to run the story only with Satyapal Singh's point of view included.

I was in the office when our resident editor, Srinivas Jain, called at about 11 p.m. Jain told me, 'Satyapal Singh had called. He raised objections to the use of the word "inquiry". The word "inquiry" in Hindi and "questioning" on the English channel sends out the wrong impression. Satyapal said that he was called to seek information, and not for an inquiry. You speak to him once.'

I said, 'I have been trying to talk to Satyapal for a while, but he isn't taking my call.' Before I could finish my sentence, Satyapal Singh called on my mobile. I disconnected Jain's call and answered his.

Satyapal Singh repeated what he had already told Srinivas Jain. 'The SIT called me to take information. The word "inquiry" used by you sends the wrong message.'

I said, 'As per my sources, you were given a list of questions and you provided answers to the same.'

The response from the other side was, 'Yes, but they are taking my help.'

'Should I run the news that the SIT took Satyapal Singh's help?' I asked.

'No, but the word "inquiry" sounds as if an alleged criminal had been interrogated. I have already spoken to Srinivas Jain.'

To Satyapal's last statement, I responded, 'All right, I will also speak to Jain. But I would have to take your reaction on camera.'

'I am busy right now. Call me at 4 p.m.,' saying which Singh disconnected.

I dialled Jain's number and briefed him on my conversation with Singh. 'We need to omit the word "inquiry". It does make the person questioned seem like an alleged criminal,' Jain said.

'So what news should we run?' I asked him.

Jain said, 'We should say a list of questions was sent to him.'

'That would also mean the same, no?' I responded.

Jain said, 'But it will be mildly diluted.'

But I had my own contention: 'Before this, the same word "inquiry" had been used for former police commissioner M.N. Singh, former DGP Subash Malhotra and T.K. Chowdhary, former home secretary Ashok Basak, Sameer Bhujbal, etc.'

Jain said, 'Sameer is still on the radar. Yes, I can understand the other two. But for now, we will say a questionnaire was sent.'

The call ended with Jain on this note.

How mere words like SIT's 'inquiry' or 'questioning' could cause harm to one's public image. For the first time, the intense realization of this fact hit me hard. Actually, the circumstances were such that many policemen had already been arrested and 'inquiry' drew a circle of suspicion around people.

The reality is, Satyapal Singh came in much later. Much water had flowed under the bridge before Satyapal's posting as the head of crime branch in 2003. According to Satyapal Singh, he was only asked 'What are the rights of

Satyapal's and Parambir's 'Inquiries'

a joint commissioner?' and 'What are the rights of DCP (detection)?'

But he found the word 'inquiry' distasteful. At 3 p.m., I received a call from Dibang from our Delhi office. Dibang headed our Hindi news channel there. Dibang said he had received a call from Satyapal Singh and repeated what Singh had already told me and Srinivas Jain. But by that time, the news had already been altered on both channels.

Almost the same thing happened with Parambir Singh. He was also sent a 'questionnaire'. (Singh became police commissioner of Mumbai at a later date. He was removed from his post owing to the controversy related to his reportee, Sachin Vaze. After being removed, he alleged how the then state home minister Anil Deshmukh used to give him a target for gang money (hafta) collection of hundred crore rupees. This matter gained much momentum and Parambir remained deeply embroiled in this controversy for long.)

IPS officer Parambir Singh was DCP (detection) at Mumbai Police Crime Branch, the same post that was later occupied by Sawant. It was during Parambir's tenure as DCP (detection) that a case related to Telgi was registered and the investigation officer reporting to Singh had not taken appropriate action against the accused. Singh was questioned on the incident of police saving Telgi.

31

Movie on Telgi

11 March 2004

Thursday

'Sanjay, this is Mahesh Bhatt. I want to make a movie on Telgi and need some information.' The call had reached me on my mobile.

It was morning and I was waiting for the bus at the bus stand to go to the office.

Mahesh Bhatt was a renowned filmmaker. I was acquainted with him.

There were two reasons for us connecting. One, as a film viewer. This may have had years of history behind it, but Mahesh Bhatt didn't know about it. The other was my being a reporter. Almost all reporters were familiar with the fact that whether it was about the Bollywood–

Underworld nexus, or morality in the movies or any other matter which had the potential to catch the world of film on back foot, questions which made people in the industry uncomfortable, it was the Bhatt brothers, Mahesh and Mukesh, who grabbed the bull by the horns and dared to tell the story. Having faced many such interviews, I had become acquainted with Mahesh Bhatt.

I had seen Bhatt in attendance at the court during the Telgi case petition hearing. In the duplicitous, self-absorbed film industry, there were few filmmakers who were as sensitive to the contemporary issues surrounding them—he was one of them.

Upon hearing those words from Mahesh Bhatt, I said, 'Bhatt saheb, I am writing a book on the Telgi scam. It has many details. Can you tell me what kind of details you need? I will give you all of them.'

Bhatt said, 'Do one thing. Whatever you have written, email it to me.'

'But the book isn't complete yet. Only 70 per cent has been written,' I replied.

'Send me however much you have written,' said the voice from the other side.

I said, 'I will mail it to you, but please do not disclose anything about the book to anyone.'

With that, I took his email ID and mailed him my book draft the same night.

Mahesh Bhatt seemed elated when we spoke again after two days. He showered me with praise for the excellent writing. When he discovered I did not have a publisher yet, he voluntarily spoke to three or four publisher friends of his, recommending me to them personally. Two or three more days passed by. He called me again and said, 'I want to make a movie based on your book. Your character will be the lead, and this movie will be about the Telgi scam exposé. It will be a fact-fiction movie.'

This was good news for me. A sensitive filmmaker such as Bhatt was showing interest in adapting my book into a movie. I had watched many movies made by Mahesh Bhatt, such as *Saransh*, *Janm*, *Naam* and *Zakhm*.

Three days later, Mahesh Bhatt called me for a meeting. At this meeting, Bhatt's daughter Pooja, screenplay writer Neelesh Misra, and two financiers were present. I was told Pooja Bhatt would direct the movie and they would purchase the film rights for my book. Irrfan Khan's name was agreed upon to play the role of Telgi. To play my character, first Ajay Devgn's and then Manoj Bajpayee's names were suggested, but we did not get consent as both had played similar characters—a righteous man from the lower middle class—in movies, earlier.

What could have been a greater source of joy for me than this? Yet, I contained my happiness. There is so much planning that happens in Bollywood, but unless the film is complete, it is best to hold your horses and not celebrate. Many such movies had been planned but never made. That's why I chose to remain quiet. The subject of my book could pose a great risk to any financier's money. The names of many powerful and elite men were associated with the scam. Especially people from the police force. It was like being at war with an opponent way mightier than oneself. Every businessman, before investing in a new project, tries to be conscious of his forthcoming interests. Ultimately it is he who has to stay and work within the system. Only a brave financier can take a risk like this. I had my own doubts on the matter, which I discussed with Mahesh Bhatt later.

I was asked the tentative date for the completion of the book. I told them, in all likelihood, two senior politicians and their relatives might get arrested soon. That would conclude this inquiry, and along with it, my book.

But nothing happens in life as planned. The same happened here. My book wasn't meant to have the ending I had predicted as the Supreme Court was about to release an important directive in this matter.

32
CBI Inquiry

16 March 2004

Tuesday

I was in Delhi that day. During the hearing of the PIL petitions filed in the Telgi scam case, the Supreme Court gave orders to transfer forty-eight out of over 200 cases listed against Telgi, to the CBI, for further investigation and prosecution of the offenders. The list of twenty-three cases related to Maharashtra included Pune's Bund Garden police station case, which was the most popular amongst all the cases against Telgi. This case had led to the major arrests of policemen and MLAs, shedding light on the mother of all scams, the Telgi stamp scam.

CBI Inquiry

It was a deeply traumatic day for the SIT. Although their investigation was almost over, the team had scheduled the last chargesheet submission by March end. Subsequently, the arrest of a prominent politician was certain in this case.

The SIT's ship sank just as it was nearing the shore.

But since cases related to Telgi had their tentacles planted in states across the country, it had acquired a national stature. The need for a detailed investigation was thus felt and bringing in the CBI was a logical progression for the investigation.

Within a few days, the CBI took all the matters into its hands.

I got a phone call from the CBI office one day. I was told DIG Arun Kumar wanted to meet me. (Arun Kumar later became joint director of CBI, additional DGP of Uttar Pradesh and Director General of the Railway Protection Force and Vice President of [UIC] International Union of Railways.)

I met him the next day. Two flats in the PWC guest house on Dr Annie Besant Road in Worli had been converted into a temporary office for the CBI team designated to manage the Telgi scam investigations. The CBI was still settling into the case and the office. Arun Kumar was known to be a sharp-witted man. The credit for killing the most dreaded gangster of Uttar Pradesh, Sri Prakash Shukla, goes to him.

Arun Kumar met me with a lot of warmth. He shared how he had finished reading my book (first edition) in one go on the previous night, and how much he had loved it. He started showering me with praise for my courageous writing, and slowly came to talk about his real motive. He said the CBI was still finding its feet in the case, but he needed help from me. He wanted me to find out if Telgi's money had been used to pay the rental for a helicopter used in eminent lawyer Ram Jethmalani's travel from Aurangabad to Dhule, to attend a programme. I asked him why the CBI couldn't find this out for themselves, as they had both the authority and the means to figure it out, while I had neither. His response to my question was intriguing.

'Jethmalani is not a lawyer, but an institution. He will entangle us so intricately, the next 200 years would be spent extricating ourselves from the maze and the case will miss reaching a logical conclusion.'

On that day, the stature of Ram Jethmalani in the legal world became evident to me. Anyhow, Kumar and I parted ways with a promise to stay in touch. Both of us had a fair notion of what things would be like, going forward ...

33

The Unresolved Questions

Ganga Prakash

The general manager of the India Security Press, Ganga Prakash, was arrested on 19 December 2003. He was later released on bail. He had been accused of illegally selling old printing machines along with negative and positive stamp designs to Telgi.

Unconfirmed information received from 'sources' was that Ganga Prakash was making all efforts to get transferred back to Nashik. Before this, Prakash, who used to be posted as deputy general manager at Nashik's India Security Press, had been promoted and transferred to Hyderabad. Both he and Telgi had wanted him to stay in Nashik. Prakash pulled out all stops to get transferred back from Hyderabad to Nashik in a few months. Many questions can be raised in such a scenario:

1. Ganga Prakash sought Telgi's help to stay in Nashik after his promotion. Following Telgi's instructions, the MLA from Dhule, Anil Gote, wrote a letter of recommendation to then law minister Ram Jethmalani to reinstate Prakash at Nashik. Ram Jethmalani gave the letter to then finance minister Yashwant Sinha. Telgi camped at Delhi along with Anil Gote till he got his way. Why was Prakash's abrupt transfer to Nashik not investigated until now?

2. How was Ganga Prakash recalled from Hyderabad to Nashik so promptly? Why were the rules broken and who decided to make an exception?

3. According to the sources, Ganga Prakash's transfer was approved by a finance ministry secretary-level official. Does this imply that an official of a higher rank than a finance secretary or some politician interfered to facilitate Prakash's transfer back to Nashik?

4. Who were Telgi's and Ganga Prakash's contacts in the elite power circles of Delhi?

5. Had this aspect been kept a secret until now to save a senior official or politician from facing the heat?

The Unresolved Questions

The questions above needed answers. For some reason, my intuition made me believe this link could uncover explosive and sensational insight into the Telgi scam case. When former law minister Ram Jethmalani fought the elections against Vajpayee from Lucknow, he gave a statement on 29 April 2004 that the stamp scam had direct links to the prime minister and his office. Disregarding all rules and official recommendations, Prakash had been transferred from Hyderabad to Nashik by the Prime Minister's Office, under pressure from MPs from the Telugu Desam Party.

The CBI paid attention to Ganga Prakash and arrested him from his home in Hyderabad. He had been accused of helping Telgi. Prakash and his associates had assisted Telgi in acquiring printing machines, sharing technical know-how and various other aspects of printing genuine stamps. After this, the old machines were handed over to Telgi without being dismantled.

A CBI spokesman shared that cases had been registered against five Indian Security Press officials and three Railway Protection Force officers. The CBI further shared that Telgi had gifted two expensive watches to Prakash in person, and Prakash had sought his help for his promotion. Later on, based on the CBI's report, Prakash was dismissed from service.

The question of officers and politicians from the Centre who were connected to this case remaining unscathed so far, still loomed large. But the pertinent question remained: what was the reason behind the inquiries of Sameer and Chhagan Bhujbal? The kind of inquiries they had been subjected to could not be compared to the questions Ashok Basak, Narayan Rane and M.N. Singh, etc. had been asked.

The SIT had endured to question the uncle-nephew duo—surely, something must have come out of it? They must have had a basis and unconfirmed evidence which had led to the questioning. Why weren't those records disclosed? How come all of it suddenly led to a dead end? Would the truth ever come out? One thing was certain, the prominent names appearing in the Telgi scam must have triggered some damage control exercise to keep the matter under wraps.

Was there a specific purpose behind keeping the matter away from people's reach? These questions were weighing on my mind. For me, it was time to reassess my journalistic values.

All this had thrown me into a state of despondency. Despite working relentlessly, all my efforts made so far suddenly seemed futile. The media may have been labelled as the fourth pillar of democracy, but I could foresee it losing its credibility. In this case, the line between news coverage and personal emotions had been blurred for me and I was struggling to overcome my disillusionment. As a reporter, certain matters overpower you so greatly that it takes ages for you to overcome the delusion. My unabated internal turmoil had begun consuming me.

I often felt journalism had no relevance. The idealism that had drawn people like me to the field seemed like a shiny mirage. My frustrations had peaked to a level where I felt disconnected from my work. Life seemed like nothing more than an empty shell.

I felt some aspects of the investigation were deliberately being suppressed or ignored. It was evident that the prolonged stretching of the matter would cause people to lose interest and reduce public awareness about the case. People would slowly start forgetting about the scam and move on. Even the media would abandon it. And on top of this would pile up the debris of long-pending high-profile cases, all lost to oblivion. All efforts, down in the dumps! Because, after all, 'justice delayed is justice denied'.

During this time, offers started pouring in for me from other news channels, promising better salary and higher positions.

My mental exhaustion, despair and frustration surged to the level where I made up my mind to resign. When I shared my intention with people within the organization, they flatly refused to accept my resignation at any cost. They counselled me to accept struggle as a way of life. Noting my failing mental health, every senior colleague advised me to take a week off to go on a holiday as I truly needed to restore my mental peace. I also felt the urge to contemplate and meditate in solitude. While sending me off for my holiday, I was told that upon return, a big responsibility awaited me—a pleasant but crucial promotion.

34

Telgi Gets Me a Promotion

'Listen! You have become the bureau chief. Got the promotion. Behave yourself now! Why are you still coming to the office in old, faded jeans? Donate those rotten shoes to the museum and start wearing dapper, branded clothes.' Cameraman Sanjay Rokde's banter from behind me pulled me out of my year's flashback. Watching Rokde drive off on his bike after his shift, I thought to myself, how time flies!

It was six in the evening. I was wrapping up work for the day.

I was felicitated for the Telgi scam exposé and tremendous reporting. NDTV was selected for the International Press Institute of India Chapter award, for reporting on Telgi and the baby-swapping racket. This was the first time this prestigious award had been bestowed upon any news channel in India. The award was conferred

Telgi Gets Me a Promotion

upon NDTV by then President A.P.J. Abdul Kalam at Delhi's Vigyan Bhavan. Before the commencement of the award ceremony, NDTV Chief Prannoy Roy told me he would receive the award on my behalf. And post receiving the award, not only did Prannoy Roy appreciate my work in his acceptance speech on stage, but he also announced that I was being promoted to the post of Mumbai bureau chief. As a bureau chief, my responsibilities and the expectations from me grew a lot. I wasn't a solo show any more. I was equally responsible for the work of the journalists reporting to me.

I stepped out of the office for a stroll and got myself a cup of tea from the tea stall. I had barely taken a sip when my mobile rang.

'Hello.' It was a familiar voice. 'It's me.' It was my source.

'Namaste. How are you?' I greeted him.

'Do you remember what day it is today?' my source asked.

'Of course. How can I forget this day!' Everything flashed before my eyes in a quick replay. 'It all started exactly a year ago, on this day. Today was the day when you handed over Subodh Jaiswal's investigation report on Telgi scam to me.'

'Yes, today was the day that set the ball rolling. Exposed the mother of all scams. So many prominent people were arrested.' The source let out a deep breath.

'Yes. Today was the day,' I replied.

'Then you must rejoice,' he said.

'But the court's verdict is still pending in that case.'

'The courts will work at their own pace. Why are you spoiling your party? You must celebrate the anniversary,' my source insisted.

'How do I celebrate?' I was clueless, what was I to do?

He could perhaps sense my predicament. 'Okay. You don't celebrate, but we have a gift for you.'

I said, 'I don't accept gifts ... You know that very well.'

'I know you don't accept gifts,' he said. 'But this is a special gift to commemorate the day.'

My source laughed and continued to tease me. 'Though this is less of a gift, more of a consolation prize. Don't you want to meet the man behind all this credit you earned?'

'What!' I exclaimed. 'You mean meeting *him* ...?' My sentence remained unfinished.

My source laughed.

'But how?' I asked, swallowing my spit.

'I can tell you who can get you the key, and who can lead you to the lock,' he said.

'Hardly a cakewalk. Why would anyone do it?'

He was sure that it was a piece of cake. 'It was all under your nose until now, but you missed it.'

'Who?' I asked.

I could not believe it when my source revealed the name to me.

'No, that is not possible. You are mistaken. I have known him for years,' I said.

'Then you also must know that as high as he is above the ground, his roots run just as deep below.' His statement had some merit. But I was still sceptical that the person who was always with me like a shadow could have had the ability to make this meeting possible and had camouflaged it so well.

But my source was serious.

'You never asked him and he never told you. In your profession, the cameraman is always an underachiever.'

I said, 'He can easily get scared out of his wits!'

'That's why you need to handle him with utmost care. My information is confirmed. His contact alone can make this possible. He has goodwill there.' The source guided me.

'Do not rush into anything … Don't even think of taking a camera along. The work will take its due course. It can happen in either two months or it could take up to a year. Another possibility is that Telgi may refuse to meet or create a mess of the whole thing. The question remains, are you prepared for possible collateral damage?'

The question had a point, because even if a meeting with the man of the hour, Telgi, was arranged, other complications might follow. Also, not getting anything on camera meant no content for the news. The only solace was the one-time opportunity to meet him face to face and interact with him. And the one who enabled the accolades and bouquets to be showered upon me was worth taking a risk for.

Sensing my long pause, my source said, 'The ball is in your court now. Whether you want to use the key or not, is up to you. The key will not walk up to you. If he had to, he would have made an offer to you already. He's been shadowing you this long without ever uttering a single word about it. The sign is clear, you will have to walk up to him.'

Triggered by a bout of anxiety and dizzying curiosity, I felt the pressure to urinate, but curbed the urge. In the next few minutes, my ramshackle motorcycle was running on busy Mumbai roads towards Tilak Nagar to meet my key. Mumbai's eastern suburb Tilak Nagar is the origin of two schoolmates associated with it. One was the crime syndicate kingpin Chhota Rajan, and the other, my cameraman, Sanjay Rokde. Now meeting Chhota Rajan wasn't possible since he was overseas, in hiding.

35

Telgi Unplugged

'So, a thirst for pussy caused all this?' (*Chut ke chakkar main?*)

He raised his eyes for the first time in the conversation, his concentration broken. Telgi hadn't seen it coming so directly. *This* daring and indecent? It put a dent.

In reality, Telgi was like a Super Tusker. Various police forces and agencies from across the country had failed to break him and extract information. He had told all investigators only as much he was willing to reveal—just enough to answer the questions asked of him and give him a breather until the next inquiry.

A man who was so adept at facing tough investigations—getting any information out of him was tough. In journalism, a twist like the one Telgi had just got is called 'giving a shock'. If a question is asked in an unexpected or inconvenient manner, keeping grace and courtesy at bay, it can rattle anyone. Like on a cricket pitch, the uneven bounce or a sudden deflection can baffle even the most seasoned batsman, similarly, a sudden or unexpected question can unsettle the seasoned player of any game.

This was the purpose behind using such crass mannerisms and language during questioning.

But the real motive behind asking such a question was to make the best of the situation and utilize a unique opportunity earned with great difficulty. The idea was to milk the maximum information from this direct conversation with Telgi.

I met Telgi twice, both within court premises. I used jugaad to reach the court passage where Telgi was scheduled to appear. Mandar Parab was with me. Two heads are better than one. Also, cameraman Sanjay Rokde was present without his camera, standing at a distance. Telgi looked directly at me for the first time and recognized me. Silent greetings exchanged through eyes.

Mandar initiated the talk with a question: 'What do you think? All these cases, how long will all this last?'

'How do I know?' Telgi's response was terse but bereft of dilly-dallying or a wilful silence. This was our unspoken invitation to ask whatever we wanted to ask him.

Sensing this, I asked directly, 'Your arrest and stamp confiscation happened before as well, but the business never stopped. What caused the obstruction this time? Got stuck in the police's internal squabbles?'

Telgi gave an unbridled response but paused after every sentence. 'Keeping it running wasn't the issue. Confiscation, arrest, court … this all is part and parcel of our business. It would have continued smoothly for years, but the police got greedy. They brought my wife and children into it. My family had no role to play in all of this. But they threatened to invoke MCOCA against them and asked for money to buy their silence. They started blackmailing me. A deal should be treated as a deal only. Deal with me, if you must. Why drag my family into this mess? If I had given the money once, the same would have to be repeated at every juncture. My family would suffer.'

Unlike his characteristic natural flair, Telgi took a pause after every word to present his thoughts point by point, and give away not just what was adequate for us, but all that he could. And that was exactly what happened.

'But why would they behave in such a manner?' My next question was a natural progression from the previous one.

There was no emotion or aggression in his voice. The response came, point by point, coherent, just like last time.

'I blew up money at the dance bar. Word got out. New policemen kept appearing. They continued to screw me like a whore. My paper was like currency too. I gave them my paper, they sold it in the market and earned money. They thought I was a fucking idiot. A small-time pickpocketing arsehole. They would take bribes and let me go.'

At Telgi's response to this second question, one could only speculate if things might still have gone out of hand had his family not been put in the line of fire.

'If they hadn't dragged your family into the matter, would things not have escalated to this level?'

His answer was direct. 'Anyone would do this to protect their family, no?'

'That means you had such prominent people incriminated in self-defense?'

Telgi was very clear. 'What would they have done to my family otherwise?'

Mandar then tried to extract a few names from him.

'You are highly connected in the corridors of power. Why would these people mess with you?'

Telgi took to his natural flair for conversation, not taking any pauses this time.

'Zero! Except for Anna, everyone treated me like a pimp. Anna took me in as his son. He was unnecessarily trapped.'

Not getting desirable answers to his question, Mandar tried a different approach, 'How did you get HIV?'

The answer was controlled, as if he had anticipated the question.

'Don't know. It's good it didn't get transferred to anyone in my family.'

When well-rehearsed answers start coming in, one has to use jugaad to rattle the interviewee. And if two people are questioning, it gives enough room to the other person to attack with an impactful counter-question, as the interviewee would still be distracted by the previous question. I used this proven strategy and asked, 'So, a thirst for pussy caused all this?'

Telgi, who had been handling all our questions with patience and self-control until now, took a long pause at this. This was not a pause in between predictable questions. This pause was to deliberate upon a strategy to answer such an obnoxious and indecent question.

My signal was direct. Tittle-tattle about his debaucherous lifestyle were common knowledge. For the first time during the meeting, Telgi turned his thick neck towards me—only his neck moved as he would've had to defy gravity to turn his massive body by 120 to 180 degrees to face me. Before responding to such irreverence, the egotistical sharp-witted men replay them in their minds.

'Are you asking if thirsting after pussy landed me here?'

'Who knows!'

He sidelined the question and turned the discussion onto me, 'I read the book. Well done ...'

Now this was a trap.

It was good feedback for a novice author's first book. Praise for a new author's writing is more enticing than any honeytrap that has ever conquered a spy. Telgi subtly moved the attention away from himself and saved himself from the obnoxious questions that may have followed, and shifted it on to me.

I asked, to satisfy myself, 'Was the writing all right?'

Now the leash was back in Telgi's hand.

'You get to know everything beforehand. You will be dragged into court for it. Not me, the police will do it.'

'You were about to write a book too.'

'I told my lawyer. A movie adaptation is planned as well.' After answering, Telgi started walking as a policeman signalled him to move along.

Mandar asked him as he was moving, 'Is the heroine duplicate story true?'

I could not gauge the expression on his face, but 75 per cent of the right side of his face betrayed a smile on his lips and he was heard saying, 'How does one get the original? Tried in Bollywood but there the Punjabi mafia thinks everyone is an ATM.'

He moved his obese frame, balancing it precariously on his parted and bent legs. Overweight people are often observed walking tilted to one side as their groin area, under the underwear, rubs against their inner thighs causing sores and rashes; so to avoid the discomfort, they walk with their legs apart, tilted at an angle.

Mandar, Rokde and I got out of the building. We jotted down the main points from the conversation in the car, analysed his words and their between-the-lines connotations. The gist was that Telgi had been blackmailed by the police, who were holding his family hostage, in a way. Telgi had caught a whiff of their scheme. The whole exposure had been made possible because of Telgi, or had gone as per his wishes. His hunters had either been hunted or were still stuck in traps. He was in great distress, but was satisfied that his family was safe. What one didn't need to read between the lines for was that if corrupt policemen had not acted greedily and laid traps to capture Telgi's family, then who knows for how many more years the stamp scam may have continued to run unobstructed.

This was the era in TV journalism when news was substantiated with evidence. Video bytes a were must. That too for a sensitive matter like the Telgi scam; if you worked at a reputed channel, the seniors would ask for a video byte first, and without it, would drop the story immediately. Looking back now, one can see the merit in this healthy practice.

But the one who noticed the most distinct point in the conversation with Telgi was Sanjay Rokde. Though he was at a distance, his experienced hawk eye, peculiar to cameramen, enabled him to develop an amazing visual sense. He drew our attention to the 'distinctive thing' that we had seen in Telgi's demeanour, especially in his later interviews or appearances on TV. Rokde pointed out that Telgi's long, flat smile and the strange combination of mischief and daredevilry reflecting in his eyes spoke volumes. They were a constant reminder that 'You all are fucked-up idiots, and even though you have caught me, your hands are still empty.'

36

The Storm That Followed the Narco CD

6 September 2006

'*Ganpati Bappa Morya!*'

The whole of Mumbai was reverberating with this acclamation. It was the day of the visarjan of the city's most beloved deity—the last day of the Ganesh Utsav, when the idols of Ganesh are immersed in the sea. In just one day, fifteen to twenty lakh people assemble at Girgaon Chowpatty. This telecast always enjoys high viewership, so all anchormen and women dress up in traditional Maharashtrian outfits and position themselves at the location from 3 p.m. onwards. Almost all news channels had sent their reporting staff to cover the event.

At that very time, one channel broke an exclusive news. Telgi's voice was heard on the TV screen saying some words like 'Mister Sharad Pawar … Mister Bhujbal'.

This was enough to raise a storm. TV reporters who had gathered to cover the Ganesh visarjan went into a helter-skelter mode. Everyone was calling me, as this breaking news was playing on my channel, Times Now. As per a pre-planned strategy, I had switched off my mobile. Only one channel hadn't dispatched their journalists to the site of the Ganesh visarjan, because it had all been strategized beforehand.

We had limited staff and so we decided to break the news at an opportune moment, when other channels were soaked in the revelry of Ganesh visarjan, from which they would take time to recover. By the time they would plunge into the matter, Times Now would be far ahead of the others. Everything happened as planned, thereafter. The agenda of the day was somersaulted and journalists decked up in traditional dress ended up losing their makeup to sweat in the seaside humidity.

Now it is pertinent to mention here that I had quit NDTV in the year 2005, and joined a new and upcoming channel, Times Now, as its deputy news editor. The Times of India group had designated former NDTV journalist Arnab Goswami to be the channel head. The paradigm shift for me occurred due to my jump from the Hindi-medium to an English news channel. Except for the Delhi bureau, all other bureaus reported to me.

The game plan was to transmute the natural pace and carry the aggression of vernacular journalism into the English news channel. That's why I recruited Hindi–Marathi journalists and over time, this proved to be successful. Another interesting occurrence was the opportunity to work with Mandar Parab for the same news organization, after a long gap of five years. Mandar joined as the chief news coordinator. Now, let us return to Telgi's narco CD news.

The journalist who had gained access to this tape, his name was Madhav Gopal Krishnan and he was the Bangalore bureau chief at Times Now. A brilliant journalist, the credit of bringing this tape within public view goes to Krishnan. It would be better if the first-hand experience of the narco test CD story is related by Madhav himself, so I am quoting the same here.

In Madhav's words,

> Bits of the information from the narco test had already been published in newspapers. So this was already a high-profile case. What had not been seen was the tape of the narco test. On that summer morning, when I got a call from a colleague that the Telgi narco tapes had been leaked, I frantically made calls to lawyers, cops, forensic experts and journalist friends associated with the case, to figure out where the leak had happened.

I finally got through to someone who had the tape. Within half an hour, we started beaming the tape through our OB van parked near the Karnataka High Court. It was an instant hit. Telgi virtually rattling off the names of the who's who of the political firmament of Maharashtra sent shockwaves. It forced big leaders to instantly deny the charges.

I got a call from a top leader in the national capital, who knew me from before, appreciating the story. More than the politics, it was the trivia surrounding the narco test that glued people to itself. Telgi slurring out big names under the influence of sodium pentothal, or the truth serum, was a spectacle in itself. In addition to that, I had people questioning me why he was being slapped around!

Many days later, when I spoke to the forensic experts who did the test, they explained that this was only a means to revive him and keep him awake while in that trance-like state. If they didn't do that, he would drift off to sleep. Also, they were constantly monitoring his vital statistics to ensure the drug had no adverse impacts on his body. The same question would be asked in different ways to see if he responds differently.

Just as Times Now ran this news, a sensational wave spread across India. It resulted in a political tsunami at a national level. All politicians were hesitant to share their reactions with the media. Sharad Pawar was a name to reckon with. He had served at various posts, from Maharashtra's chief minister to roles at the Centre in various cabinet positions. Sharad Pawar had been friends with every national or regional party in India. He was the chief custodian of the NCP in the NCP–Congress coalition government.

Currently, he was heralded as the saviour and anchor of the Manmohan Singh-led government at the Centre. In or outside power, everyone from Maharashtra's bureaucracy to its police force was under Pawar's control. The pulse of Maharashtra's politics was in the hand of the almighty Maratha stalwart Sharad Pawar.

Perhaps that was why clarification and damage control was done so rapidly.

Declaring this as irresponsible and baseless, Sharad Pawar said, 'I'm not at all connected with this. The CBI never called me for investigations. But I will not mind further probe. I am told that the tests on Telgi were carried out three or four years back, and after that the investigating agencies have carried out their probes. No one at any time made any inquiries with me. I was also not part of the government at that time.'

Let me clarify, when Pawar said he was not part of the government, he was referring to the Central government, where he became cabinet minister in the year 2004. In 2003, the NCP party led by Sharad Pawar was part of the government in Maharashtra.

The Storm That Followed the Narco CD

This might bring some respite to a big leader like Bhujbal that the name of a leader above him was embroiled in the controversy. Bhujbal nixed Telgi's statement, telling the media, 'Telgi is a rogue. I don't have any idea why he dragged Pawar saheb's name into this. What I understand from his connivance is that he is trying to escape from his crime. After all, this test was conducted three years back. Naming big politicians is his strategy to create pressure on us or this is his idea of seeking revenge. You have to remember that the narco test was conducted in Karnataka and the findings need to be validated. In the end, when questions were raised regarding the role of Karnataka's politicians in the scam, he dawdled and circumvented the question. And then he takes our names. This shows his shrewdness. How can one accept his statement as authentic?'

The matter was related to a cabinet minister. The CBI also released a statement. CBI spokesperson G. Mohanti stated, 'The narco analysis test on Telgi was conducted by SIT, Pune, at the Forensic Science Laboratory (FSL), Bangalore. The CBI never conducted this test on him. We had received the recording of the test when the case was transferred to the CBI in 2004. The CBI pursued all leads from the test, but did not find any corroborative evidence against the two politicians.'

CBI sources also informed us that Telgi had told the CBI investigators after the case had been transferred to them that he had deliberately lied in the truth serum test, so that he could divert the attention of the investigators, as the whole case was solely focused on him.

After two days, Telgi's written statement was released through his lawyer, Harshad Nimbalkar. He stated that he never took the names of Sharad Pawar and Bhujbal in the narco test. Along with that, Telgi denied ever meeting or paying any money to either Sharad Pawar or Bhujbal. Telgi said the video footage shown on TV was distorted, fabricated and doctored. That means the tape was manipulated and the content was changed.

Telgi said the tape shown on the news channel was not the original narco test footage or CD. However, there was a contradiction in Telgi's statement. Telgi stated he did not take any names, which was a blatant lie, because both the video and the CBI had said Telgi took the names. On one side, he was saying that the original video had been tampered with. On the other side, he was also saying that a clipping was not part of the original video. Both things could not be true at the same time.

This controversy also gave birth to self-appointed experts who raised questions on the authenticity and credibility of the narco test. For this reason, it is crucial to understand how the narco test works. The narco test is done to extract truth from an accused or a criminal. In this test, the criminal or accused is administered an injection of a psychoactive medicine called truth serum or sodium thiopental or amobarbital. This causes their active mind to go into a state of sleepiness. Which means that the person's logical skills are suppressed, and the person reaches a stage somewhere between sleep and wakefulness. He is neither sleeping, nor fully awake. (The readers are requested not to confuse it with a drunken state.) Post this, questions are asked to extract the truth. In the state of partial fainting, the accused unwillingly blurts out the truth. During the test, the investigation officer, doctor, forensic expert and psychologist are present.

It is important to intervene here and share that there is no sure-shot way to guarantee that the accused/criminal will reveal the truth during the narco test, and that the case would be solved.

Sometimes, the accused/criminal is a big crook and can befool the investigating team. It is imperative to share that the success of narco tests depends on what kind of questions are asked. Narco tests definitely help the police and the CBI in certain crucial cases. Bangalore SFL director B.M. Mohan shared in an interview that the narco analysis helped police in 95 per cent cases to get crucial evidence.

In this case, another accused and former MLA Anil Gote demanded a narco test to be conducted for Sharad Pawar and Bhujbal at a Pune trial court, which was not taken seriously.

Another speculation was also doing the rounds. Many believed this gave Telgi room to bargain, so that he could bring someone to the negotiation table for his important arrangement.

The main thing was that the media quelled the issue. The politicians' statements were accepted as gospel truth.

Within forty-eight hours, both the news and the news follow-up were hushed up.

TV channels and newspapers both suddenly turned their face away from the news. Even our own channel Times Now went quiet on this subject within a day and no follow-up news or investigation followed. It wasn't a natural silence. In journalism, pin-drop silence like this is not considered natural.

But also in journalism, the editor's word is considered as the final word, so we all agreed to comply. But a ray of hope was still flickering at the end of the tunnel, that could possibly light up a fire.

37

I Did Not See Telgi Alive after This

After September 2006

'The names you took in the CD, was that correct information?'

The most hard-hitting and direct question had been asked. If the response had been in the affirmative with details, ripples would have been felt not only in Maharashtra but throughout the country.

But in response, there was only a smile. It was an indication in the beginning itself that the conversation was going to be brief, pensive and one-sided, to a great extent. One cannot help but wonder that there must have been some limitations somewhere—no one turns unfaithful without a reason.

'Why have you suddenly turned cold?'

An emotionless smile in response, yet again. This state of no reaction was worse than 'no comments'. A challenging and instigating question had been posed, but Telgi had ducked it.

This was the second meeting with Telgi. Once again in the court premises; once again, Mandar was with me and cameraman Rokde stood without his camera, at a distance.

When the probability of getting any long and detailed answers out of him started diminishing, I asked him another question for which a yes or no would have sufficed: 'Is the settlement done?'

But he gave me no answers. Just a long, deep silence. In limited-overs cricket, if the batsman leaves one ball after the other to pass, then it must be inferred that the match has been fixed, but one must not give up until the last ball for that reason.

'Meaning?' There was no hope of getting any answers to this question either, but we did hear a mumble in response.

'I am destined to die here [in jail]. But the rest have been secured.'

He gave his response in two sentences. First, dying in jail was Telgi's certain fate. But then what was the 'rest' that had been safeguarded? What had been saved? We had surmised it, but Mandar tried to get a clarification from him, 'Rest meaning family?'

'Wife does not keep well. The daughter will be married off in some time.' His answer cleared the mist from the question. The deal was sealed on his family's safety and their future was secure now. In return, Telgi had turned the gun on himself.

'Meaning nothing new will come out now?'

'You have already exposed so much. Is that not enough?' He implied from this statement that somewhere we also needed to put a full stop on our work, because against Telgi's wishes, nothing could ever come out.

This strengthened the belief that whatever may have happened, even as all the strings unravelled, one string was always in Telgi's control.

'Got any guarantee?'

'The word is all that matters in dealings.'

Telgi's answer translated to this that since he had agreed to cooperate verbally, there was no need for a written pact. In such a scenario, the question brewing in my mind was, in case anything happened to Telgi, would his family continue to be safe?

After all the sacrifices that he had made for his family, what if they were still targeted or scapegoated after him? Or left in the lurch to fend for themselves? Then what would happen? Had Telgi prepared a backup blueprint—an insurance or a plan b to ensure his family's safety? And keeping this in mind, I asked Telgi a question that no one in the world can answer.

'What is the guarantee after you are dead?'

'No fucking guarantee.'

Vicious mind. He played my trick from the last meeting on me, this time. In a conversation, let the quality of your language drop so low that the attention of the other person shifts from the content to your language. An unexpected answer violating all codes of decency, the unbridled aggression in the response evidently a warning that what was going to follow would not be pleasant. Once civility was out of the window, you could ask whatever you wanted to, but at your own peril.

When the person in front of you is treading upon firmer ground, rather than turning against him, it's better to let him gloat in his little world and worship the ground his feet tread upon. As a seasoned reporter, Mandar knew this, so he asked him what Telgi was waiting to hear.

'A win in a way?'

Telgi did not say anything. Looking at Mandar, he nodded his fat neck in affirmation.

'Was it easy?' Mandar continued his questioning.

Telgi responded, 'This is my world now.'

This was an unclear response, but the best possible conclusion one could derive from this was that he knew there was no chance of escaping jail any more and the rest of his life was fated to be spent attending court trials and serving jail terms. He was mentally prepared to endure it all. And based on this assumption, I asked, 'Have you made arrangements inside?'

'It is all right.' A brief, frigid and terse answer affirmed the following: 'A hassle-free, comfortable and functional lifestyle had been arranged for within the jail premises.'

'Mobile inside?'

'No.'

I Did Not See Telgi Alive after This

The odds of Telgi's response in this case being a lie were pretty high, because why would he disclose to us if he had access to a mobile? He had lied about this to many officials who had investigated before. Though convicts being in illegal possession of mobiles within the jail premises is nothing to be surprised about. It happens.

'Why did you change so many lawyers?'

'Where is the money to pay them all?'

I posed a counter-question to Telgi's response, to ask if he actually even paid anyone at all that he would allow their payments to remain pending.

'Then, what did you give them? Goli (sugar pill)?' The meaning of 'goli' in this question was, 'Empty talks, or a placebo, false hope or like an invitation that read "welcome to fuckery"'.

'Business proposal and property.'

If the readers of this book understand dark humour, then they must have concluded by now that Telgi's 'business proposal and property' was like a special 'supernatural' power that lured people towards itself only to disappear, and the people chasing this illusion ended up making fools of themselves. These people included politicians, police, journalists, lawyers and bureaucrats.

In reality, there are only two omnipresent elements that are yatra, tatra, sarvatra (here, there and everywhere): One is God, the other is chutiyapa (bullshit). Every person has both within them. You spend a lifetime searching for one, and the other finds you on its own. As the proportion of one's influence in your life increases, that of the other correspondingly decreases.

'Only goli then?'

He did not respond but it was evident he was laughing; his stomach was jiggling, threatening to spill out through the buttons of his tight shirt.

'What about the book and movie?' This question was more to satiate a personal curiosity than journalistic angst.

'Not fixed.' His words were sweet as honey to my ears. I heaved a sigh of relief as Telgi was a bigger authority on himself and his information would have been far more valuable than mine in this matter.

It was also cleared up that as far as his comments about penning a book on his life and making a movie on it were concerned, they were like his stamp papers which were manufactured by an authentic machine (straight from Telgi's tongue) but were fakes.

He gave such statements only with the intent to keep prospective authors or filmmakers at bay from writing or making movies based on his life, as no one would be able to compete with the authenticity of his own writing which he claimed that he would bring out.

After all, the original was an original, even if it was based on the life of a fraudster named Telgi. My sources tell me how he never completely settled the bills of all the lawyers who fought his various cases. In lieu of paying their fees, he served them big dreams (business proposal, property, book and film rights) and availed their services at a discounted fee.

Watching Telgi depart in a police van, I thought about how we had met Telgi twice. But in reality, we had met two different Telgis in two different meetings. The Telgi from the first meeting was impetuous but satisfied, sadistic, had mischievous eyes and appeared nonchalant about his future. Telgi of the second meeting was dejected, paralysed, an average criminal who made a compromise with his nemesis—detached but with a focused gaze.

The first one's gait showed pride and confidence, the second one's, lethargy and submission. The first one concealed hidden messages in between his words and the second one weighed every word, chewed on it, before spitting it out to us.

Our cameraman Sanjay Rokde had drawn this analysis. The cameraman's thinking aids his ability to visualize and as a senior mediaperson, Rokde has a fantastic ability to draw conclusions based on visuals, much more so than many reporters.

The eloquent Rokde had a polite, courteous and diplomatic demeanour that gave him the harmless appearance of an affable and benign person, thus, at times, his sources turned out to be better than the sources of reporters. I have absolutely no hesitation in accepting that both the meetings with Telgi were organized by Rokde through his own sources, a feat that many big reporters had failed at.

But there was one thing we noticed only when Rokde pointed it out, which was that both times, a circle was visible on Telgi's pant cloth under the zip. This had formed due to urine incontinence.

It was apparent that Telgi had been keeping unwell and due to his high diabetes, his ability to control his urine had reduced, leading to leakage and the formation of the wet circle under the chain of his pants. Another reason for Telgi's deteriorating health could be his mental state of surrender and abandon.

In conclusion, we could rationalize that Telgi's final settlement was done. The policemen allegedly conspiring to illegally trap his family and extract money from him caused all hell to break loose. Now as per the deal, Telgi's family would be kept out of the mess and would likely not be troubled in the future.

In exchange, Telgi would put a leash on his shenanigans—meaning that the names of prominent people and big personalities would remain under wraps and those 'influential people' could enjoy a good night's sleep after a full day politicking and policing, peacefully. Telgi would comfortably live in jail for the rest of his life and die there, too. His compromise sealed his fate because there was such a plethora of legal cases pending against him in so many courts that it was practically impossible for him to ever get out and live as a free man again.

On top of all this, he was suffering from a chronic, life-threatening disease which was adding greatly to his

I Did Not See Telgi Alive after This

discomfort day upon day. Given such a scenario, he did whatever he could have done, to the best of his ability.

Our inferences were confirmed when the CBI made his wife a co-accused, but made getting her out on bail easy. A man who had been in judicial custody for years, who was destined to stay in jail indefinitely, and who was now dying from an incurable disease—for him, meeting his family at regular intervals could be a boon to his otherwise painful existence.

This was not the end of Telgi as a man's story only ends in his coffin. But it was indeed the end of the Telgi scam. After this, counterfeit stamps were neither printed nor confiscated, will not be printed or confiscated. The cases will go on, till they get judicial closure.

Now, no more reports would leak, no more narco test videos would come out, no more lie detector tests, and no possibility for the unspoken truth to come out of the long chargesheets.

Telgi, who gave this scam its monumental stature, had doused the fire and destroyed his own scam. The scamster had lost the battle to the family man. Telgi's scam was over but Telgi had remained. Though he was alive, our second meeting was our last with Telgi.

I had seen him face to face, breathing, for the last time. I did not see Telgi alive after that day.

38

Who Was He?

Second Week of September 2006

Mushrif was sitting stoically in his chair in a hotel room in Pune that day. His trained police eyes were scanning the room for a hidden camera, so that before or after the interview, during off-the-record informal conversation, he was not camera-trapped into saying something that could be detrimental to his career.

Doing a 360-degree review of the room assured him that there were only two cameras there. These were not CCTVs, but regular, big commercial-use cameras.

I had persuaded him to appear for an interview the right way. So far, whenever he had been seen on TV it was either at the court or another public place, where mics were thrust in front of his face for his bytes for brief moments. But no regular interview had ever been conducted.

The level of research and exemplary reporting done in the Telgi case by yours truly must have strengthened his confidence in me that I would not botch up his interview. But owing to the compulsions of a policeman's nature, the suspicion and mutual mistrust came out by force of habit, as was expected from him. I did not mind his eyes surveying the room for hidden cameras.

Though I never joined the bandwagon of sting operation journalists, I did plan to entangle Mushrif the regular way. This plan was crucial for arriving at the reason for why the way a name that had come up in the Telgi CD was quashed, raising questions about the statement of the accused.

After that, it was imperative to keep the debate open on that one name, with a person whose credibility would be much higher than that of the statement made by a known criminal.

Although questions would be raised on Mushrif as well, as the political machinery was already in place for rebuttal or suppression of his statements—giving excuses like groupism in the police force or labelling it as a vengeful act driven by the angst of a frustrated police officer—but despite all these predicted hurdles, it was important to rekindle the fire and get the debate going. Mushrif's interviews so far had mainly covered the merits of the case, opposing policemen and statements related to the home ministry.

He never made any comments on the politicians. It is not that politicians wouldn't have approached him on this matter directly or indirectly—it is difficult to digest this fact, especially since his own brother was a minister in the coalition government and willingly or unwillingly, politicians and policemen do cross paths and get acquainted.

As it is, Mushrif's base was Pune and those who understand Maharashtra's politics would be well versed with the fact that the capital of Maharashtra may be Mumbai, but Pune was its power centre. Political ideology of the ruling NCP–Congress coalition state government flowed from Pune to Mumbai.

It was worth taking a chance. A room was hired at a Pune hotel. The set-up for the interview was complete.

At the sound of 'rolling', I began the series of questions and answers. This was the era when journalists could not be seen shouting at or ridiculing their guests.

The intention of the question–answer session was to maintain a decorum and mutual respect while deriving some news, without causing any commotion. I started with some heartwarming questions that weren't meant to extract any news. Mushrif became comfortable and eased into the questioning. Then, I came down to my real self.

First and foremost, Mushrif gave a balanced response on a question related to Telgi's narco test. 'We can be certain that the names revealed by Telgi hold some significance. But the agency must examine every important lead found in the narco analysis test. This is a scientific test and must be given its due importance. Otherwise, what is the point of conducting the test?'

Question: When you were part of the investigation, did you suspect the involvement of any politician?

Mushrif: The direction of the investigation did give signals of something being out of place. Upon my request for the removal of the investigating officer, officers from the rank of assistant commissioner of police to inspector general of police stood up against me, which wouldn't have been possible without a solid backing.

Question: So much was going on. The internal conflict matters of Pune Police were coming out in the open. Sometimes policemen, at times their cronies, were holding press conferences. You too were in combat mode. In between all this commotion, did any neutral person or man of authority try to intervene and resolve the conflict?

(Mushrif hesitated.)

'Yes' or 'no', both would be big news, but a 'yes' would carry more weight. Mushrif took an extraordinarily long pause that lasted for two or three seconds. These two or three seconds may seem like a small unit of time to the reader, but in the world of TV journalism, it holds significance.

I could confidently say that the answer was a 'yes'.

Now, Mushrif could say 'no', but if 'no' was the answer, he would have answered instantly and not taken such a pregnant pause. Typically, the interviewer repeats his question in case his guest missed any part of it the first time. After a pause of two to three seconds, Mushrif said, 'There was an attempt.'

I stayed quiet. Mushrif broke his silence again.

Mushrif: At the onset of all this, I received a message one day and then on the next day, at seven in the morning I reached 'hostel' and a meeting was held there.

(Here, 'hostel' does not refer to a student's hostel, but the designated place in Pune to meet the politician for this meeting.)

Question: Who were they?

(Mushrif was silent.)

Question: What happened at the meeting?

(By now, Mushrif had recovered from the contingency and regained his composure.)

Mushrif: It was about this matter.

Question: What was said?

(Mushrif was silent again.)

Question: Means there was an intercession?

(Mushrif was silent.)

Now was the time to implement 'plan b', because Mushrif had probably decided not to give any more details. So whatever remaining details or signals could be extracted had to be pulled out now. Something was better than nothing. I skirted around the clues to identify the politician in question and relay the news to my audience. Though I knew it was a politician, I still asked.

Question: Was it a politician?

Mushrif: Yes.

Question: This politician … is he from Maharashtra?

Mushrif: Yes.

Question: Is the politician from West Maharashtra?

Mushrif: Yes.

Question: Is the politician associated with the ruling party?

Mushrif: Yes.

Question: Does the politician have a good hold on the ruling coalition in Maharashtra?

Mushrif: Yes.

Question: Would this politician have any connection with the Telgi scam or the other accused in the case?

Mushrif: Could be.

Question: Does this politician have political interest in both the state and the Centre?

Mushrif: Yes.

Question: Does this politician currently hold power or has held it in the past, in the state and the Centre?

Mushrif: This is way too direct.

Question: Does he control power in sugar cooperatives, sports, administrative organizations, sports administrative bodies?

Mushrif: Please stop now.

The interview was concluded. Though not all of it could be used, there was enough ammunition here to create news and reinstate the debate on the Telgi scam. After watching this interview, one could easily assume the name of the aforementioned politician.

Upon my return from Pune, I wrote the report the very next day and edited the video. Then I sent the news to my boss and the editor. Colleagues like Mandar Parab, Ketan Bondre, Kamlesh Sutar, Nikhil Dixit, Anant Sonwane also read this report.

Everyone was excited about it as it poured fuel into the tank of a car stuck in no man's land. We could take the statement given by Telgi with a pinch of salt as it was the statement of an accused, but these indicators had come from a responsible policeman, the one who in many ways, could be considered the original whistleblower in the case.

He had put his own career and his minister brother Hasan Mushrif's political career at stake by agreeing to give this interview.

But there was no decision taken on when and how the sensational interview would be aired. Today, tomorrow, next week … the dilly-dallying continued. Each time, a different reason was given. This continued for two weeks and the excuses for the delay continued to change.

I relentlessly kept following up. Asked in person, sent reminder mails. Sometimes objections were raised, calling it a hidden agenda of Mushrif's.

At times, questions were asked such as why he had not taken the name directly. Everyone could understand the manipulations at work but was also aware of the unreasonable, unpredictable and vengeful behaviour of the editor.

Though there were doubts that the editor was talking on behalf of the management, he did not want to dilute his larger-than-life image by portraying himself as the management's pet, so under the 'best served cold' policy, he continued to act evasively.

My patience was wearing off as time passed. Mushrif was also following up regularly on the date the interview would go on air. Each time, I gave him a new date, also preparing him for the eventuality that the possibility of it not being aired at all was there, given how it was diminishing. Mushrif had braced himself for the impending storm. He was waiting: when would the dam break? Slowly, Mushrif also realized that the telecast was not going to happen.

What Mushrif, my colleagues and I had suspected had come true. Though it wasn't rejected officially, the airing was put on hold unofficially for an indefinite period.

Mushrif gave me an earful on the phone. He did not accept any of my explanations. I had also lost a source in Mushrif in the process. He did not speak to me for years after that telephone call and I also did not have the courage to call him. Because, in some way, this topic would have arisen between us and I would have had to bear the embarrassment all over again.

Overall, everything was diverted into a single direction. First, Telgi's narco test report and then the follow-up report on the CD case became a no-go zone for the media.

Then, the second meeting with Telgi gave loud and clear reaffirmations of the same and now, the abortion of Mushrif's interview was also emphasizing the same thing which is usually explained with much love in north India in words like, 'Let it go, motherfucker. Nothing more can be done now.'

At a personal level, this was a time of deep despair. Mandar Parab and other friends of mine stood by me, but my heart felt detached and disillusioned.

Eventually, I mailed my resignation to the company's HR head Zahira Crosta on the afternoon of 14 October 2006. Journalists usually send their resignation to the editor, who then forwards it to the HR department. The reason being that an editor is an institution in himself in the world of journalism.

But in my immediate world, that institution had already collapsed, that's why I deliberately did not send my resignation to Arnab Goswami, the editor, so that it sent out a strong message and became a symbolic expression of my displeasure at their handling of the matter. The editor and company requested me to withdraw my resignation, but I stood my ground and bid farewell to Times Now.

39

Downfall of Journalism

The water was flowing in full force showing no signs of stopping. The non-stop torrential downpour had created a situation of floods in the city. The pouring skies showered not water, but calamity. The city hadn't experienced torrential rains like this in a decade.

Mumbai was drowning, over a thousand people had died, people had lost their homes, cars had been flooded. 26 July 2005 has gone down in history for this reason. Something else began on the same day that was historic: the downfall of TV journalism.

Actually, the downfall of journalism is a continual process, where the decomposition slowly occurs as the body ages over time. But the floods of 26 July added fuel to the fire and hastened its arrival in TV journalism.

For the first time in TV journalism, the drama element was foregrounded. On TV news channels, people separated from their loved ones or those stuck in the rains connected 'live' with their loved ones, and TRPs skyrocketed. More TRPs meant more advertisements. After successfully running the pilot trial of this formula, a new channel was crowned as the number one channel. All other channels jumped on the bandwagon.

Every channel was doing the same thing. Suddenly, the fights between spouses, conflicts between children and their parents became a commonplace view on TV. People from both sides would go live on TV and fight. There would be an outpouring of emotions. People would feel entertained. Couples in love started landing at TV stations.

In the coming months, a seasoning of entertainment was sprinkled on top of this drama. Until now, Bollywood or entertainment reporting that had been on the sidelines became mainstream. It became a priority.

In the midst of news channel programming, entertainment-related content increased exponentially, be it the saas–bahu soaps, standup comedy or dance reality shows ... all came into vogue as they promised high TRPs.

In the next two years, gaucheries like Rakhi Sawant and Raju Srivastava began to be considered tasteful. From hunting down of animals to snakes mating, everything was telecast. Somewhere, a man was surviving only on ice, somewhere else, a woman was living on a diet of salt.

Partial clips of sex scandals were played, from the paranormal to sex experts, who came on air late in the night, everything found a place in TV journalism. Unconfirmed videos sent by anyone from anywhere were being played on TV.

It all happened at such a fast pace that mainstream reporting, political news, investigative journalism and the news that actually mattered was pushed to the margins. The government was only too happy with the shift. Any government would be elated that the public was engaged in mindless entertainment rather than paying attention to real and burning matters that concerned the nation.

For those who had embraced journalism to bring about some change in society, this was no less than a fall from grace.

In the future, whenever the history of TV journalism would be written, it must be registered that on 26 July 2005, the virus of bullshit penetrated news channels, and has been eating the system from the inside-out and strengthening itself ever since.

If you were troubled by devoted journalism and screaming, shouting anchor-men and anchor-women, then please know that the seeds of this decay had been sown many, many years ago.

I joined IBN7 after quitting Times Now, and then News-X. During my schooldays, I had to work as a paperboy, delivering newspapers to people's homes, and after becoming a journalist, I had found a way to do the same job of conveying news to them through their TVs.

During the Telgi scam coverage, I had rejected many offers, ranging from a Honda City to a famous heroine.

I willingly restricted my personal freedom. I ducked honeytrap calls from unknown numbers and struggled to remain unscathed. Only to land into this mess after. A small part inside of me cursed me for not accepting the lucrative offers.

The idea of journalism had completely changed from what we had envisioned. This was a very frustrating situation for me as I felt like an odd one out in the current context in journalism, and my heart was falling out of love with reporting.

Escapism is good, at times, just like that ad which says 'stains are good'. It was an opportune time for me to take a break.

I left my job. I completed my PhD and to satiate my wanderlust, and I set out on a year-long India tour. I travelled in sleeper class and motorcycle. Slept anywhere from rest houses to benches on railway platforms, and travelled the entire country. I returned and tried my hand at teaching journalism, but I was quite average there. I joined Zee News, eventually, and stayed there until 2020. During this time, I also studied law.

After the news had been suppressed the last time, my heart lost all attachment to the matter and I never reported on the Telgi case ever again. Though in the downfall phase of journalism, no new revelation or sensational reporting came to light in the Telgi-related cases.

Whatever happened later was only natural progression, like Telgi's remand transfer, next court date, how much punishment in which case and his deteriorating health.

The CBI's investigation moved at a snail's pace. Everything felt scripted. No speed, no swiftness, no new disclosure and no big arrests.

Imagine if a car driving at the speed of hundred kilometres per hour under the SIT was reduced to ten kilometres per hour under the CBI, questions are bound to a rise. Yet, there were no new recoveries, the whole attention was directed on pursuance of matters already listed, wherein scams like these are like chains, with every link leading to the next, and that was just what had happened in the last five years, but was not to happen any longer.

40
Order, Order ...

Time elapsed and different cases continued on their own trajectories. One of Telgi's brothers, Abdul Azim, MLA Anil Gote and IPS officer Sridhar Wagal and a few more accused were released on bail. Some others were discharged, including R.S. Sharma, DCP Pradeep Sawant and Inspector Vasisth Andhale. A few others like Sawant and Datta Dhal were reinstated in the police force. Telgi remained in jail.

When his mother, Sharifa Bee, passed away, Telgi was allowed to travel to Khanapur for performing her last rites. Telgi's elder brother, Abdul Rahim, had passed away a few years back. His daughter Sanna got married in the year 2014. Telgi got a day's furlough from jail to attend his daughter's wedding. Telgi's son-in-law, Irfan Talikoti, had a silk export business and was also the Youth Congress head at Khanapur.

Of all the related matters in court, some are still ongoing and decisions have been given in a few others.

Out of the cases in which the court passed its directives, a verdict given by the Pune court is worth mentioning here.

The biggest surprise element was Telgi's change of heart while taking the stand. He pleaded guilty and made an emotional appeal in front of the judge, with folded hands. 'I have good faith in the judiciary. I am suffering from diabetes, heart disease, kidney problem and both my legs are paralysed. I need an urgent kidney operation. My health is deteriorating day by day. My wife is ill and on her deathbed. My only daughter is of marriageable age and no other male member is there in my family. I pray for minimum sentence. I am penniless and cannot pay the fine. I have been in judicial custody since 7 November 2011. I pray for leniency.'

The judge responded to his appeal, 'It's only because you have repented that you have got a lenient punishment. If you had opted for a trial, you might have been more severely punished.'

The verdict by the Pune court sent everyone into a spin. In its orders for one of the cases, the Pune court levied a penalty of 202 crore rupees on Telgi and imprisonment of thirteen years. If Telgi was unable to pay this amount, then another three years and three months were to be added to his term of imprisonment. This was perhaps the highest penalty against an individual in the history of the Indian legal system.

Besides this, the verdicts were out in many cases and some others were still under trial. Let us take a look at the main points in cases where verdict was passed:

- In the 1992 fake stamps and fake passport case, five people, including Telgi, were sentenced to a punishment of five years' imprisonment.
- In the case related to Christopher Bhatti's murder, who cheated and stole from Telgi, four people including Telgi were given punishment of seven years' imprisonment and a fine.
- In one case from Nashik, from 2005, Telgi was given a punishment of ten years' imprisonment and nine lakh rupees in fine.
- In a 1995 case, Telgi, his accomplice Sanjay Gaikwad and guru Ram Ratan Soni, were sentenced to ten years' imprisonment.
- In a case from Karnataka, Telgi and seven others were sentenced to seven years' imprisonment in one case.
- In a case from 1999, where forty-seven lakh rupees worth of fake stamps were found on Mira Road, close to Mumbai, the guilty were sentenced to seven years in prison and a fine of twenty lakh rupees.
- In Bangalore, Telgi and two doctors were sentenced to seven years' imprisonment in a case of fabricating a medical certificate. Telgi was also fined twenty-five lakh rupees, while the two doctors of government-

run Victoria Hospital were fined fourteen lakh rupees each.

- In a 1999 case of selling counterfeit stamp papers to banks and private firms worth lakhs of rupees, a court in Bangalore sentenced Telgi and four of his accomplices to imprisonment for ten years.
- In a 2001 Delhi case of fake stamp papers worth 212 crore rupees, Telgi was sentenced to seven years' imprisonment and 1.3 crore rupees in fines.
- In the seventy lakh rupees worth of fake stamp paper seizure cases registered at Colaba and Cuffe Parade, Telgi, his accomplice and guru Ram Ratan Soni, three police officers and one government official were convicted in the year 2012. The special courts of Mumbai passed a judgement sentencing Telgi to lifetime imprisonment.

Few of the aforementioned punishments were to appear concurrently, and a few others, separately. In total, Telgi was already looking at thirty years in jail. In most of the cases, Telgi confessed to his crime and that became the basis for the verdict.

The crucial question that remains is what could have caused a change of heart in a fraudster like Telgi, who went on a confession spree after having embarked on a tirade of accepting his crimes?

I have tried to answer this question in the last few chapters. But when this unbelievable phenomenon repeated itself back to back, TV journalism, on its way down, did not attempt to dissect it or try to 'read between the lines'.

Earlier, different sets of lawyers at different times used to represent Telgi and share his piteous state, talk about the problems faced in jail, lack of medical treatment, a larger conspiracy, big names, Telgi being made the scapegoat, Telgi being made the sacrificial lamb—all those kind of things were heard, but no such speculations are heard now.

This kind of silence is deafening. In the times of the downfall of journalism, the investigations into the Telgi scam were symptoms of the decay. These lines from the famous Hindi poet Dushyant Kumar's poem come to mind:

Yahan tak aate aate sookh jaati hain kai nadiyaan,
Mujhe maloom hai paani kahan thehra hua hai.

Many rivers dry up before they reach this point,
I know where the stream of the water is stuck.

41

What Is Yours, to You …

Last Week of October 2017

- Cardiac disease
- Hypertension
- High blood pressure
- Trouble in breathing
- Kidney disease
- Multiple-organ failure
- Heavily uncontrolled diabetes
- Meningitis
- Limited mobility

And who knows how many more ailments plagued the body of the man lying in the ICU. The voices of his daughter and son-in-law reached his ears, 'Your granddaughter is waiting for you to get better and is eager to meet you.'

Unable to say anything, a tear falls from Telgi's right eye on to the pillow. He has no recollection of how he reached the ICU of Bangalore's Victoria Hospital. He was twenty kilometres away, locked up in the Parappana Agrahara Central Jail, serving his thirty years' term in prison.

Everything was all right until three months back. In his jail cell, there was a cot, an LED TV, a can of filtered water and two tables. He needed protein to fight disease, so home-cooked food, including eggs and chicken, was made available for him on a regular basis. A fellow convict was his masseuse, to massage his hands and shoulders.

He was unable to walk and moved around in a wheelchair. Three or four fellow convicts visited him in his cell, to help him move around or offer any small assistance that he may need.

In the same jail, Tamil Nadu's political prisoner Shashikala, too, was kept in relation to a disproportionate assets case. During an inspection of the jail, DIG Rupa found that prisoners like Telgi and Shashikala were leading a life of luxury. So she made a report on this.

She mentioned in her report how three or four prisoners were employed in giving them massages and running errands for Telgi. DIG Rupa stated that Telgi was all right and could move around easily on his own. When the news spread, to carry out damage control, the DIG's boss, DGP H.N. Satyanarayan Rao, gave a statement that DIG Rupa was not well versed with the jail rule book. To counter DGP's claim, a CCTV footage was leaked which showed

Telgi sleeping in his cot, an LED TV in his cell, a jar of potable water, two tables and a prisoner moving to and fro in his cell.

On this, the jail's chief superintendent gave the clarification that there was nothing illegal or out of place in the tape, because there is no restriction of movement inside the jail or helping other prisoners on humanitarian grounds.

Most of these convicts knew each other and some were serving sentences for the same case. 'As per a directive from Karnataka High Court, keeping Telgi's deteriorating health condition in mind, he must be provided with a wheelchair, medicines and diet advised by the dietician. Telgi cannot walk even ten metres without assistance now.'

But despite this clarification, a storm erupted. In the media, that video made for headlines like 'Telgi's opulent lifestyle in jail' because in comparison to the deplorable conditions our jails are in, what Telgi was getting was no less than five-star treatment.

There was no shortage of convicts in bad health, but despite that Telgi had managed to get whatever he needed to survive, and this showed how, irrespective of the condition he was in, he had still managed to pull stunts like this.

Anyway, DIG Rupa was immediately transferred. The Karnataka government transferred four more senior officials, including DGP Satyanarayan Rao—who was accused of accepting bribes in lieu of providing the facilities in custody.

In reality, this whole drama was politically driven and played out in July 2017, keeping in mind Shashikala, who was a politician and a big leader of the All India Anna Dravida Munnetra Kazhagam (AIADMK) from the neighbouring state of Tamil Nadu.

As the saying goes, 'when bulls fight, the crops suffer'. The same thing happened to Telgi. He got caught in a street fight and had to let go of his comforts. This affected his resolve of 'dying in jail in peace and rest'. His health started declining within a few weeks.

In the second week of October 2017, his health quickly deteriorated. Initial treatment was given by the prison medico, but it did not help. On 13 October (Friday), it was discussed that Telgi must be shifted to a hospital, but he asked to be moved after two days, on Monday. On 16 October, Telgi was moved to the hospital.

On 19 October, his condition worsened and he was put on ventilator. Inside the hospital, Telgi's condition was worsening, but outside, his family was not ready to give up on him. Telgi's son-in-law was a constant presence at the hospital, on the ready to look after his father-in-law.

Telgi's daughter, Sanna, told the press, 'The doctors may not be promising anything but I know my father is a fighter and he will be all right very soon.' Telgi could have been anyone in the world, but for his daughter, he was the world's best father. Telgi's wife, Shahida, was fervently praying for her husband's good health at her brother Abdul Salam's house in Bangalore.

She stood by Telgi in his good times and bad times. She raised their daughter almost as a single parent. She was also made an accused in the Pune case, and yet she had no complaints of Telgi.

In the dargahs all across Telgi's village, from Rajasthan's Ajmer Sharif to Karnataka's Khwaja Bande Nawaz, his friends and family were praying for his health. But the almighty had stamped death on Telgi's forehead. On 26 October 2017, 3.55 p.m., Telgi breathed his last after multiple-organ failure.

On 28 October 2017, an ambulance that came from five hundred kilometres away in Bangalore carried the dead body of Telgi, which was handed over to his family after the post-mortem. Telgi's younger brother, Abdul Azim, stepped up to receive his brother's body from the ambulance but his daughter, Sanna, humiliated him and tried to stop him from becoming part of Telgi's funeral procession. In front of the large crowd, a bitter fight broke out between Azim's and Sanna's family.

Abdul Azim was Telgi's younger brother. He had spent five years in jail along with Telgi in the stamp scam case. After coming out, he had chosen politics as his career and was elected the president of the Khanapur City Nagar Palika, Khanapur town municipality.

Sana forbade Abdul Azim and everyone from his family from lending their shoulder to Telgi's bier or attending his burial. Telgi's wife, daughter and son-in-law complained that Abdul Azim collected wealth and properties worth crores of rupees, but did not support Telgi in jail during his bad times.

Abdul Azim tried hard to explain that despite his multiple efforts, he was not allowed to meet Telgi in Bangalore Jail. The scuffle got out of hand and two sons of Abdul Azim's tried to attack Telgi's son-in-law, Irfan. But the police intervened at the right time and prevented a violent outburst. The matter was settled only after Abdul Azim left the place with his family and the final rites were carried out.

About two thousand people joined Telgi's funeral procession. Some were people from his ancestral village, Telgi, Bijapur, that became enmeshed with his identity. Khanapur, where he helped people get jobs, gave them money to start their businesses, donated money for the upliftment and maintenance of temples, mosques, dargahs, contributed to weddings of the poor, social programme sand sporting events. The same Khanapur also had people who had taken advantage of Telgi in his heyday, but did not bother to attend his funeral.

At the Khanapur Bahaar Gali Mosque, Namaz-e-Janaza was read and a prayer of forgiveness for Telgi's crimes was recited. Then his janaza was taken to the burial grounds outside the city's periphery. Abdul Azim again reached the graveyard and the commotion restarted.

Finally, the elders counselled Abdul Azim and convinced him to leave, after which the burial ceremony started, which was completed by Telgi's son-in-law, Irfan. At 2 p.m., Telgi was returned to the care of the earth (supurd-e-khaak).

All the money, all the help he gave to people, did not serve him as his family could not live in peace even after his death. Maybe Telgi had an inkling of this. Any man who spent his last few years in bad health and in a bleak future before him would have envisioned death lurking at his door for years, and dreaded what lay ahead.

This was why he shared his last wish only with his wife. After the last day of the mourning period post his demise, Telgi's wife and co-accused Shahida, made an application in the courts and shocked everyone when she shared Telgi's last wish.

As per Shahida, Telgi's last wish was that all the properties in his name or his benami properties were to be confiscated by the courts and used for social causes in national interest. Shahida submitted the list of immoveable properties and benami properties he had bought in the name of his relatives which had not been confiscated by the CBI as yet. The list included seven properties in Belgaum and two in Bijapur, including thirteen flats, thirteen shops and 6.5 acres of land in Khanapur, valued at approximately more than a hundred crore, which the CBI had no clue about.

Shahida said in court, 'I am a God-fearing woman. It makes no difference if a person goes to heaven or hell after death; every person is awarded punishment for his bad deeds on this earth itself. My faith in life teaches me only one thing: do right and stay away from sin.' If Telgi had understood what Shahida had said in court years ago at the beginning of his own criminal journey, then probably all that happened may not have happened at all.

Shahida's case continued. Away from the limelight in the big cities, Shahida died on 3 August 2022 in Khanapur. There is no burden on her soul as she returned what did not belong to her. What is yours, to you …

Epilogue

A folklore from the Middle East, Europe, Egypt, India and China mentions a mythical bird called the phoenix. The size of an eagle, this multicoloured bird is said to resurrect itself from its own ashes upon its death. When people think the bird is dead and has turned to dust, it is reborn from its own ashes, which is why it is also known as a magical bird.

Telgi was also like a magical bird. Whenever people thought he was done and dusted, he rose from his ashes, to come alive once again.

When his father died, the responsibility of running a family fell on his shoulders, when he was just a young schoolboy. Acquaintances and relatives in his village in Khanapur did not offer him any support, but he soared regardless. He educated himself, and went to Mumbai and the Middle East to work.

When he went to prison for the travel agency fraud, his sole means of livelihood was lost, and who would give employment to a convicted felon? At rock bottom, he acquired a new skill in jail, and this was the beginning of the stamp scam.

Between 1999 and 2001, he was arrested multiple times by Andhra Pradesh Police and Karnataka Police, thus exposing his scam. He was thrown into a jail in Karnataka. But just as the policemen thought Telgi's work was done, to everyone's surprise, he continued his scam from jail, and only made it bigger.

When Maharashtra's Pune Police force caught him running the racket from custody, it was felt that now his end was near, but it was just the beginning. Telgi collaborated with his investigating police officers and continued his scam with their help.

When the world-famous Mumbai Police caught a whiff of his scam, they grabbed his neck and captured him, at which point it seemed like the country's most professional and dreaded police force would finally put a stop to Telgi's scam. But instead of doing that, he diversified into a new direction, and was again saved.

When his alliance with Mumbai Police was caught by the Maharashtra and Karnataka SITs, it seemed his game had finally come to an end.

When the SIT report suppressed by the Maharashtra home ministry was exposed and the scam was revealed to be much larger and widespread—the mother of all scams—causing many big names to get dragged into the controversy, one assumed that surely, now everything was over. But the government dismissed everything on the basis of a DIG's report. And Telgi once again escaped.

If I can get a bit philosophical and quote Murphy's Law here that states 'Anything that can go wrong will go wrong', I would extend it to a more apt version: 'Anything that can go wrong will go wrong, and at the worst possible time, in the worst possible way, and so wrong that it will be beyond damage control.'

The ship often sinks near the shore. So, when Telgi and his associates had let their guard down, the most decisive moment came. The matter went to the high court through a PIL, after which a retired senior officer, S.S. Puri, was made the new in-charge of the SIT, and an officer who was on the margins throughout his police career, dealt blow after blow along with his team to Telgi, who could never recover.

Any possibilities of the rebirth of Telgi's scam ended there. The Telgi scam was finally over. Telgi might have been alive but without his scam; he was like a gun without a bullet—only iron. This scam gave birth to Telgi, who cast his net throughout the country, endured so much humiliation, braved rounds of torture, developed animosity against people with far greater power and scammed them.

One cannot see the scam and Telgi as separate from one another. The scam was Telgi's will to live, to change the world, to immortalize his name in the world, but Telgi dissolved with it.

Eventually, he returned where he had started—the basic criteria for being considered a good human, that is, being a good son, a good brother and a responsible father. Telgi spent the last ten years of his life patiently waiting for death to knock on his door. In those final moments of his life, he ultimately decided to have all his earnings from the scam to be used to further national interests.

There may be multiple fake document scams prevalent throughout India and the figures may reach lakhs and crores of rupees, but there will always be only one Telgi scam in which counterfeit documents were printed on real machines with real printing blocks. Lakhs of deals, transactions, purchase of properties and affidavits are still in existence and have not been declared illegal or unauthorized.

That means the impression left by the Telgi scam on the lives of crores of people, without them ever realizing which one of their official paperwork was made on Telgi's papers and which one on the government's. Trying to tell the difference between the two is as arduous as trying to distinguish a bear's pubic hair from the rest of its fur.

About the Author

Sanjay Singh is a senior television journalist. Investigative journalism is his favourite line of work. In his twenty-five-year-long exemplary career, he has worked with news channels such as Zee News, NDTV, Times Now, IBN7 and News-X.

Sanjay exposed the Telgi scam, among many other big scams in the country.

The web series *Scam 2003: The Telgi Story* is based on this book and has been produced by Applause Entertainment with filmmaker Hansal Mehta as the showrunner.

Also, while a web series is being planned based on Sanjay's book with Rakesh Trivedi, *CIU: Criminals in Uniform* (2023), another has already been adapted from his book based on the sensational killing of Sheena Bora, *Ek Thi Sheena Bora* (2023).

In addition to being a law graduate and having a doctorate from Mumbai University, Sanjay is an academician associated with various educational institutions.

About the Translator

Gayatri Manchanda is a New Delhi-based translator, artist, bilingual writer, content developer and lyricist. A nomadic traveller and photography enthusiast, she made a transition to the world of writing after two decades of corporate stint across hospitality, global mobility and real estate. Her work includes two books of assisted writing, audio stories and fiction write-ups in magazines and newspapers.

30 Years *of*

HarperCollins *Publishers* India

At HarperCollins, we believe in telling the best stories and finding the widest possible readership for our books in every format possible. We started publishing 30 years ago; a great deal has changed since then, but what has remained constant is the passion with which our authors write their books, the love with which readers receive them, and the sheer joy and excitement that we as publishers feel in being a part of the publishing process.

Over the years, we've had the pleasure of publishing some of the finest writing from the subcontinent and around the world, and some of the biggest bestsellers in India's publishing history. Our books and authors have won a phenomenal range of awards, and we ourselves have been named Publisher of the Year the greatest number of times. But nothing has meant more to us than the fact that millions of people have read the books we published, and somewhere, a book of ours might have made a difference.

As we step into our fourth decade, we go back to that one word – a word which has been a driving force for us all these years.

Read.